# ONE-DAY DIY

## MODERN FARMHOUSE FURNITURE

# ONE-DAY DIY

## MODERN FARMHOUSE FURNITURE

Beautiful Handmade Tables, Seating and More
*the Fast and Easy Way*

**JP STRATE & LIZ SPILLMAN**
***Founders of*** ⌂ **THE REHAB LIFE**

PAGE STREET
PUBLISHING CO.

PAGE STREET
PUBLISHING CO.

First published in 2020 by
Page Street Publishing Co.
27 Congress Street, Suite 105
Salem, MA 01970
www.pagestreetpublishing.com

Distributed by Macmillan, sales in Canada by The Canadian Manda Group.

24   23   22   21   20      1   2   3   4   5

ISBN-13: 978-1-62414-933-7
ISBN-10: 1-62414-933-2

Library of Congress Control Number: 2019942676

Cover and book design by Rosie Stewart for Page Street Publishing Co.
Photography by Kate Becker© and JP Strate and Liz Spillman

Printed and bound in China

# DEDICATION

*JP:* To my parents, the biggest influences in my life:
Bernadette and John


*Liz:* For Schmoopy

# CONTENTS

# INTRODUCTION

Hello! If you are reading this, chances are you are someone who is interested in DIY, but don't have a ton of time to invest in projects that take weeks to build or require a garage full of fancy tools. Well, lucky for both of us, you have picked up the right book! We are JP and Liz of The Rehab Life. We started out as home remodelers who, along the way, began a YouTube channel showing viewers how to make their own furniture and home decor. We wrote this book to expand our vision of making DIY accessible to the average person. We do this with approachable one-day woodworking projects—yes, you really can make your own dining table in a day with limited tools and no prior experience!

Don't worry if you don't have a dedicated craft room or your only reference for a biscuit is something you eat with gravy. We use simple woodworking techniques to guide you through projects for your entire home. We believe that anyone can build furniture! This is evidenced by the hundreds of messages we have received from people all over the world who went from never picking up a tool to building their own farmhouse table for their family. These messages, and the feelings of happiness and pride that they convey, are what drive us to keep creating content for beginners. It's the same feeling that we hope you will have after working through the projects in this book.

Aside from that amazing feeling of accomplishment, there are lots of reasons to go the DIY route when it comes to furnishing your home. DIY allows you to custom-build for your particular space, it guarantees that your pieces will be unique—no more generic box store decor—and . . . drum roll, please . . . it's cheaper than buying! That last reason is what originally got us into DIY! We are home renovators by day and, as any realtor will tell you, a staged home sells faster than an empty one. Armed with this knowledge and a very limited budget, we decided to build a few simple pieces of furniture for staging. Well, it turns out that building your own furniture is pretty addicting!

We now have enough furniture to stage multiple projects at a time and fill our own homes with DIY pieces. Now we want to show everyone how fun and easy DIY can be. Over the next 6 chapters, we are going to build gorgeous modern farmhouse furniture. We love this design style for its clean lines and versatility and because it's perfect for beginners. If you're ready to join in the fun, grab your tools and get ready, because the next time someone asks you where you got that cool bookcase or custom kitchen island, you're going to be able to say, "I built it!"

J.P. Liz

# HELPFUL TIPS

Okay, first things first! We know you're excited to get started, but take a quick look at the following info. It provides useful knowledge to help you on your DIY woodworking journey ahead.

## COMMON TOOLS AND MATERIALS

Here is a list of tools and items you'll be using for the builds in this book. We've tried to keep the list as basic as possible, to make the projects affordable and easy to build. I mean, really, who wants to spend $400 on a specialty tool you'll use once in your life? At that point, you might as well just buy the furniture! Even if you don't own a saw, many home improvement stores will cut the pieces for you. You probably have almost everything else laying around your house somewhere or have a friend that does!

- Brushes
- Circular saw
- Drill and drill bits
- Drop cloths
- Hairpin legs (these can be easily found online at very affordable prices!)
- Miter saw
- Pencil
- Rags
- Rubber gloves
- Safety glasses
- Sanding block or electric sander
- Screwdriver or impact driver
- Tape measure
- Trim-head screws (length depending on the project)
- Wood filler
- MDF board (medium-density fiberboard—a versatile building material)

## STAIN

Many of our projects involve staining, which adds color and gives the builds a finished look. One of our favorite shades (as our YouTube viewers can confirm) is "Honey." We use it in almost all of our builds and it can be seen in the projects throughout this book. Its rich color is neither too light nor too dark. It's perfect, really. Speaking of perfect, you'll want to keep your pieces in great shape for a long time. After all, you built them and you should be proud! Polyurethane will help protect your builds from spills, wineglass rings, pets . . . basically life. You definitely want a can handy for your projects. You may even want to add additional coats of polyurethane to those high-traffic pieces, such as kitchen tables, towel bars and coffee tables, to provide an extra layer of protection.

## LUMBER

For all of the projects in this book involving lumber, we use standard pine boards. Of course, you can select any type of lumber that best fits your taste and home; this won't change the building process described in our tutorials! Pine boards, however, are easily found at home improvement stores and are the most budget-friendly choice. When selecting your lumber, try to find the straightest boards you can. Hold the board out in front of you and eye it up and down the edges and sides. If you don't see any bowing, crooking or kinking, then you've probably got your hands on a good piece!

Now that you found a good piece of lumber, make sure you're buying the correct size. Did you know a 2 x 4 isn't actually 2 by 4 inches? It used to be, but not anymore. Today, a 2 x 4 is measurably smaller than that. The same goes for every other cut of lumber. Confusing, right? Well, we're here to help! The nice little table that follows gives you the actual dimensions of every common cut of lumber and will help guide you while building the projects in this book.

| NOMINAL SIZE | ACTUAL SIZE |
|:---:|:---:|
| 1 x 1 | ¾ x ¾" (2 x 2 cm) |
| 1 x 2 | ¾ x 1½" (2 x 4 cm) |
| 1 x 3 | ¾ x 2½" (2 x 6.5 cm) |
| 1 x 4 | ¾ x 3½" (2 x 9 cm) |
| 1 x 6 | ¾ x 5½" (2 x 14 cm) |
| 1 x 8 | ¾ x 7¼" (2 x 18.5 cm) |
| 1 x 10 | ¾ x 9¼" (2 x 23.5 cm) |
| 1 x 12 | ¾ x 11¼" (2 x 28.5 cm) |
| 2 x 2 | 1½ x 1½" (4 x 4 cm) |
| 2 x 3 | 1½ x 2½" (4 x 6.5 cm) |
| 2 x 4 | 1½ x 3½" (4 x 9 cm) |
| 2 x 6 | 1½ x 5½" (4 x 14 cm) |
| 2 x 8 | 1½ x 7¼" (4 x 18.5 cm) |
| 2 x 10 | 1½ x 9¼" (4 x 23.5 cm) |
| 2 x 12 | 1½ x 11¼" (4 x 28.5 cm) |

## PREDRILLING

Predrilling is the process of drilling a hole into your lumber where you want to put a screw, before putting in the actual screw. This will help you out with the builds in this book, and we have outlined where to do so. Predrilling not only acts as a guide and makes it easier to screw, but it also helps prevent the wood from splitting. When predrilling, choose a drill bit slightly smaller than the width of your screws, to ensure a tight and secure fit. The following table outlines what size of drill bit to use based on your screw size. Softwoods are used for all of the builds in this book and include pine, white wood, construction lumber, plywood and MDF. If you want to get fancy with your builds and use oak, mahogany, cherry, maple and so on, then you'll find yourself in the hardwoods column.

| Screw Size | Softwoods | Hardwoods |
|:---:|:---:|:---:|
| #1 | $1/32$" (0.8 mm) | $3/64$" (1.2 mm) |
| #2 | $3/32$" (2.4 mm) | $3/64$" (1.2 mm) |
| #3 | $3/64$" (1.2 mm) | $1/16$" (1.5 mm) |
| #4 | $3/64$" (1.2 mm) | $1/16$" (1.5 mm) |
| #5 | $1/16$" (1.5 mm) | $5/64$" (1.9 mm) |
| #6 | $5/64$" (1.9 mm) | $3/32$" (2.4 mm) |
| #7 | $5/64$" (1.9 mm) | $3/32$" (2.4 mm) |
| #8 | $3/32$" (2.4 mm) | $1/8$" (3 mm) |
| #9 | $3/32$" (2.4 mm) | $1/8$" (3 mm) |
| #10 | $7/64$" (2.8 mm) | $1/8$" (3 mm) |
| #11 | $9/64$" (3.6 mm) | $5/32$" (4 mm) |
| #12 | $1/8$" (3 mm) | $9/64$" (3.6 mm) |

And there you have it, you're all set to begin your journey into woodworking! Don't worry, we'll be here every step of the way with our step-by-step instructions. Good luck!

# Chapter 1

# LOVE YOUR LIVING ROOM

The living room is oftentimes the busiest room in the house and the one that requires the most furnishing. If your living room is too empty, your home will lack a cozy, inviting feel. In this chapter, we guide you through four projects to transform your living room into a warm and welcoming space for everyone.

We start you out with one of the essentials: a coffee table (page 17). A living room doesn't feel complete without one. This project, like every project in this book, is meant for beginners and can be made with just a few easy cuts and simple joinery techniques. Once you've built the top, it's simple to attach the hairpin legs, which can be ordered online or found at many hardware stores. Once completed, lay down a rug and position it in front of your couch or between two chairs facing each other and you have just created a cozy gathering space!

Two of our favorite pieces in this chapter are the Midcentury Modern Bookcase (page 23) and the Cozy Corner Blanket Ladder (page 29). We love them because they provide functional organization and, once decorated, add warmth and texture to your living space. These are easy builds, requiring just a few pieces of lumber, and while not necessary to a living room, they add so much character!

Most of the pieces in this chapter have clean lines with slim profiles, which pair nicely with a variety of decor. For a modern farmhouse look, we style them with simple accents, with an emphasis on natural materials and live greenery.

*We love this coffee table project! It's a super simple, modern design that looks great with almost any decor! The slim profile and hairpin legs allow this piece to fit well in smaller spaces, while the metal legs tie in perfectly to a lofty, industrial space. Super versatile, right? We used pine boards for the base and protected them with polyurethane so your coffee table doesn't end up with coffee stains. Get ready— you're about to create your next favorite living room piece!*

# URBAN LOFT COFFEE TABLE

DIMENSIONS: 46½" L X 24" W X 17½" H (1.2 M X 61 CM X 44.5 CM)

LUMBER (WE USE STANDARD PINE)

1 X 12, 8' (2.4 m) long (x2)

1 X 2, 6' (1.8 m) long (x2)

Tape measure

Pencil

Safety glasses

Miter saw

Drill

1½" (3.8-cm) trim-head screws

Screwdriver or impact driver

Wood filler (to match your stain color)

Sanding block or sander

Drop cloth

Rubber gloves

Rag

Stain

Brush

Polyurethane

4 (16" [40.6-cm]) hairpin legs with included screws

## STEP 1

Grab your tape measure and pencil and mark off the cuts of lumber you'll need for this project as described below. Make sure to put on your safety glasses and use your miter saw to make the necessary cuts. If you don't have a miter saw, many larger home improvement stores will cut the pieces for you.

Cut the 1 x 12s into two 45" (114.3-cm)-long pieces and four 22½" (57.2-cm)-long pieces.

Cut the 1 x 2s into two 46½" (118.1-cm)-long pieces and two 22½" (57.2-cm)-long pieces.

## STEP 2

Place your two 45" (114.3-cm) pieces of 1 x 12 side by side so they touch.

## STEP 3

Lay your four 22½" (57.2-cm) pieces of 1 x 12 side by side across the top so they are covering the two 45" (114.3-cm) pieces of 1 x 12 underneath.

## STEP 4

Predrill eight holes about 1" (2.5 cm) deep through each 22½" (57.2-cm) piece of 1 x 12 (one in each of the four corners and one in the middle of each side of the four sides) so four holes go into each 45" (114.3-cm) piece of 1 x 12 underneath (thirty-two holes total). Use your screwdriver or impact driver to secure each 22½" (57.2-cm) piece to each 45" (114.3-cm) piece underneath with a trim-head screw in each predrilled hole.

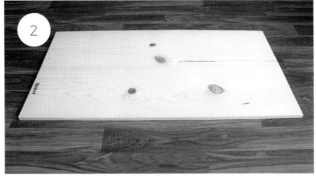

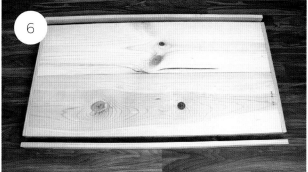

### STEP 5

Flip your framework over and place a 22½" (57.2-cm) piece of 1 x 2 flush against each short end; we're going to make a border around our coffee table. Predrill three holes through each 1 x 2 into your framework (one on either end and one in the middle). Secure the 1 x 2s with a trim-head screw in each predrilled hole.

### STEP 6

Take your two 46½" (118.1-cm) pieces of 1 x 2 and place one flush down each long side of your framework. Predrill five holes through each 1 x 2 into the framework (one on either end, one in the middle, one between each end and the middle). Secure these 1 x 2s with your trim-head screws to complete your border.

### STEP 7

Fill all of your exposed screw holes around your border by applying wood filler with your fingertip. Once it dries, use your sanding block or sander to smooth out any rough edges and remove any excess wood filler.

## STEP 8

Unroll a drop cloth to protect your floors and put on some rubber gloves to protect your hands (sorry, we're overly protective). Dip your rag into the stain and give your tabletop an even coating. Wipe away any excess. Once the stain is dry, take your brush and apply a coat of polyurethane. Watch out for drips! Let the polyurethane dry for the allotted time suggested on your can. Once it dries, you can dispose of your drop cloth or save it for your next project.

## STEP 9

Lay your tabletop so it's upside down. Place a hairpin leg in each corner just inside your 1 x 2 border. With your pencil, mark the holes where the screws will be. Remove the legs and predrill the marked holes about 1" (2.5 cm) deep. Don't drill too deep; you don't want the holes coming out the other side. Place the hairpin legs back and secure them to your framework with the included screws.

## STEP 10

Flip this guy over and whadaya know, you have a new coffee table! Center it over your favorite area rug next to your cozy couch and watch the compliments come flying in.

*If your book collection is starting to pile up, you'll want this project in your life! It's a unique build, with multiple compartments for books, pictures, plants, you name it. The long, low design, combined with sleek lines give it a midcentury modern feel, while the natural wood adds warmth and charm. To us, this is what a modern farmhouse is all about: simple, functional design using natural materials built for today's modern life. We're both avid readers and love it when our hobby can double as decor.*

# MIDCENTURY MODERN BOOKCASE

DIMENSIONS: 48" W X 25½" H X 11½" D (1.2 M X 64.8 CM X 29.2 CM)

LUMBER (WE USE STANDARD PINE)

1 x 12, 6' (1.8 m) long (x3)

2 x 10, 4' (1.2 m) long (x1)

1 (2' x 4' [61 x 121.9-cm], ¼" [6-mm]-thick) sheet of plywood

Tape measure

Pencil

Safety glasses

Miter saw

Drill

1½" (3.8-cm) trim-head screws

Screwdriver or impact driver

Wood filler (to match your stain color)

Sanding block or sander

Drop cloth

Rubber gloves

Rag

Stain

Brush

Polyurethane

### STEP 1

Grab your tape measure and pencil and mark off the cuts of lumber you'll need for this project as described below. Make sure to put on your safety glasses and use your miter saw to make the necessary cuts. If you don't have a miter saw, many larger home improvement stores will cut the pieces for you.

Cut the 1 x 12s into three 46½" (118.1-cm)-long pieces, two 24" (61-cm)-long pieces and two 10⅞" (27.6-cm)-long pieces.

Cut the 2 x 10 into one 44½" (113-cm)-long piece.

You won't need to cut your plywood; it's already the right size.

### STEP 2

Take one 46½" (118.1-cm) piece of 1 x 12 and center it over your 44½" (113-cm) piece of 2 x 10; there should be 1" (2.5 cm) of overhang on all sides. Predrill six holes (one on each corner and two in the middle) about 1" (2.5 cm) deep and secure the two pieces together with your trim-head screws. Set this aside for now.

### STEP 3

Now take your two 24" (61-cm) pieces of 1 x 12 and one 46½" (118.1-cm) piece of 1 x 12 and arrange them on end in an "I" formation. Make sure the 46½" (118.1-cm) piece is centered in the middle of each 24" (61-cm) piece. There should be 11⅝" (29.5 cm) of space on each side.

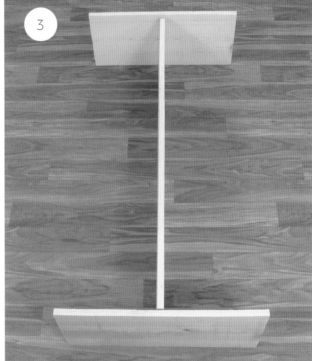

## STEP 4

Predrill three holes in each 24" (61-cm) board so they go into the 46½" (118.1-cm) board (each end and middle). Secure the "I" together with a trim-head screw in each predrilled hole.

## STEP 5

Now take your two 10⅞" (27.6-cm) pieces and place one on each side of your "I." Place them so there is 10⅞" (27.6 cm) of space from your 24" (61-cm) top board and 10⅞" (27.6 cm) of space from your 24" (61-cm) bottom board. Predrill three holes into each piece through the 46½" (118.1-cm) board (each end and middle) and secure with trim-head screws.

## STEP 6

Complete your framework by taking your remaining 46½" (118-cm) piece of 1 x 12 as well as the one with the 2 x 10 attached and placing them on either side of the "I." Predrill two holes through these two boards into each 10⅞" (27.6-cm) inner piece and secure with screws. Predrill six holes (three on each end) through each of the 24" (61-cm) boards into each 46½" (61-cm) board and secure with screws as well.

## STEP 7

Grab your wood filler and use your fingertip to dab a bit of the wood filler into each screw hole so it's covered completely. Once the wood filler is dry, use your sander or sanding block to remove any excess wood filler, rough spots and sharp edges.

## STEP 8

We're headed for the home stretch! Roll out a drop cloth and put on your rubber gloves. Dip your rag into your stain and apply an even coat to your bookcase. Let your bookcase dry completely.

## STEP 9

Once the stain is dry, use your brush to apply a coat of polyurethane. Let it dry for the allotted time suggested on your can. Once it is completely dry, you can dispose of your drop cloth or save it for your next project.

## STEP 10

Place your 2' x 4' (61 x 121.9-cm) sheet of plywood flush over your framework. Predrill five evenly spaced holes through the plywood into each 4' (121.9-cm) side of your framework border and three evenly spaced holes into each 2' (61-cm) end of your framework border. Use trim-head screws to secure the plywood to your framework. Isn't it great not having to cut the plywood?

## STEP 11

Find a wall in your living room that needs a little love, the one that you're never quite sure what to do with it. Take down your old Billy Bass and show off your new bookcase instead! It's a showcase build that will be sure to have your friends asking, "Where did you buy that wonderful piece?"

*This is one of our favorite projects because once completed, it makes it so easy to infuse color and seasonal decor into your living room! A "ladder" might sound like a complex project, but you'll use just two pieces of lumber and some straight cuts, and assembly is a breeze. Once you're done, choose an area of your living room that could use some jazzing up and add your favorite blankets. The rungs are sturdy enough to hold everything from the heavy winter blankets we Minnesotans need to light throws for our tropical-climate friends. Swap out the blankets based on the season—we love to display bright, cheery colors in the spring and summer, and chunky blankets in jewel tones in winter months.*

# COZY CORNER BLANKET LADDER

DIMENSIONS: 72" H X 21" W X 2½" D (1.8 M X 53.3 CM X 6 CM)

LUMBER (WE USE STANDARD PINE)

2 x 3, 8' (2.4 m) long (x1)

2 x 3, 6' (1.8 m) long (x2)

Tape measure

Pencil

Safety glasses

Miter saw

Drill

2½" (6.4-cm) trim-head screws

Screwdriver or impact driver

Wood filler (to match your stain color)

Sanding block or sander

Drop cloth

Rubber gloves

Rag

Stain

Brush

Polyurethane

### STEP 1

Using your tape measure and pencil, mark off five 18" (45.7-cm) sections on your 8' (2.4-m) piece of 2 x 3. Put on your safety glasses and use your miter saw to cut the five 18" (45.7-cm) pieces. These will be your ladder's "rungs." If you don't have a miter saw, many larger home improvement stores will cut the pieces for you.

### STEP 2

Lay out your two 6' (1.8-m) pieces of 2 x 3 on end; these will be your ladder's "sides." Place your five rungs in between them, leaving 10¾" (27.3 cm) of space between each rung as well as from the top and bottom.

### STEP 3

Predrill holes going through your ladder sides and into each rung. You should drill four holes for each rung (two per side about 1½" [4 cm] apart). Secure the ladder sides to the rungs using 2½" (6.4-cm) trim-head screws in your predrilled holes.

## STEP 4

Dip your finger into your wood filler and cover up your exposed screw holes. Once the wood filler is dry, use your sanding block or sander to eliminate any rough areas and excess wood filler on your ladder.

## STEP 5

Time for that glorious stain! Make sure to lay down a drop cloth to protect your floors. Put on some rubber gloves, dip a rag into your stain and apply a coat evenly to your ladder. Once the stain dries, seal it with a coat of polyurethane: Take your brush and apply the polyurethane in a smooth and even manner. Watch out for drips! Let it dry for the allotted time suggested on your can. Once it is completely dry, you can dispose of your drop cloth or save it for your next project.

## STEP 6

Stand your ladder up and you're all done! Place your new ladder in a corner of your living room that screams "cozy," hang up your favorite blankets and you'll be all ready for cuddling up on your next movie night.

*When we set out to design a TV stand, we knew we wanted it to be sleek and modern. To achieve this look, we went with clean lines and hairpin legs. It's not an overly complex project. You'll be able to build this in just a few hours, including drying time for the polyurethane. But don't let this fool you; the solid wood frame and metal hairpin legs will support your television and accessories. Although we no longer need to house bulky VCRs, some electronic storage is still needed (NES Classic, anyone?). We added enough space to balance the electronics with some decor, such as books, a plant, or for a retro feel, your DVD collection.*

# BINGE-WORTHY TV STAND

DIMENSIONS: 48" W X 18¼" H X 15½" D (1.2 M X 46.4 CM X 39.4 CM)

LUMBER (WE USE STANDARD PINE)

1 x 8, 8' (2.4 m) long (x2)

1 x 12, 10' (3 m) long (x1)

Tape measure

Pencil

Safety glasses

Miter saw

Drill

1½" (3.8-cm) trim-head screws

Screwdriver or impact driver

1½" (3.8-cm) drill bit

Wood filler (natural color)

Sanding block or sander

Drop cloth

Rubber gloves

Brush

Polyurethane

4 (6" [15.2-cm]) hairpin legs with included screws

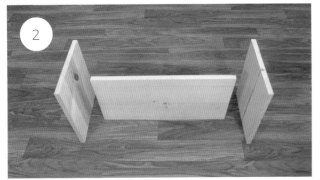

## STEP 1

Grab your tape measure and pencil and mark off the cuts of lumber you'll need for this project as described below. Make sure to put on your safety glasses and use your miter saw to make the necessary cuts. If you don't have a miter saw, many larger home improvement stores will cut the pieces for you.

Cut the 1 x 8s into a total of four 48" (1.2-m)-long pieces.

Cut the 1 x 12 into three 13¾" (34.9-cm)-long pieces, one 48" (1.2-m)-long piece and one 22⅞" (58.1-cm)-long piece.

## STEP 2

Arrange two of your 13¾" (34.9-cm) pieces of 1 x 12 so they're standing on their 11¼" (28.5 cm) wide ends with your 22⅞" (58.1-cm) piece of 1 x 12 in between the two, standing on its edge, longways. It should look like a sideways "I." Make sure the 22⅞" (58.1-cm) piece is placed so there is an equal amount of space on both sides of your 13¾" (34.9-cm) pieces.

## STEP 3

Predrill two holes through each 13¾" (34.9-cm) piece into the 22⅞" (58.1-cm) piece, one on each end. Secure the "I" together with a trim-head screw in each predrilled hole.

## STEP 4

Place your "I" on its side so it's resting on edges (the middle piece should be off the ground). Now take your third 13¾" (34.9-cm) piece of 1 x 12 and place it on its edge, 22⅞" (58.1 cm) away from your "I." Place one 48" (1.2-m) piece of 1 x 12 on its edge above these pieces. It should match up with your three 13¾" (34.9-cm) pieces as well as the 22⅞" (58.1-cm) horizontal piece.

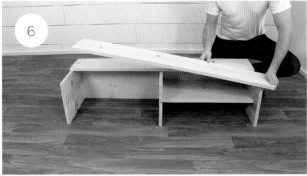

## STEP 5

Predrill three holes through your 48" (1.2-m) piece into each 13¾" (34.9-cm) piece (one hole in the middle and one on each end for nine holes total). Secure the framework together with a trim-head screw in each predrilled hole.

## STEP 6

Now take two of your 48" (1.2-m) 1 x 8s and place them flush across your framework.

## STEP 7

Predrill two holes about 6" (15 cm) apart through each 1 x 8 into each of the 13¾" (34.9-cm) pieces (six holes total). Also, predrill two holes through your 1 x 8 on the backside into the 48" (1.2-m) piece so they're spaced evenly between each of the 13¾" (34.9-cm) pieces. Secure the 1 x 8s with a trim-head screw in each predrilled hole.

## STEP 8

Perfect, let's do that again! Flip your TV stand over and repeat Steps 6 and 7 with your remaining two 48" (1.2-m) pieces of 1 x 8. It's kind of like a real-life version of pressing rewind and play on your remote!

## STEP 9

Take your drill and 1½" (3.8-cm) drill bit and make two holes through the back of your TV stand on the left side, one for each shelf. These will allow you to feed cables through your TV stand.

## STEP 10

Unscrew that wood filler and apply it with your fingertip to cover up any exposed screw holes. Once that dries, use your sanding block or sander to eliminate any sharp edges, rough areas and excess wood filler.

## STEP 11

Lay out a drop cloth, slide on some rubber gloves and grab your polyurethane. Use your brush to give your TV stand a shiny coat of polyurethane. This will give it an awesome natural look yet still provide a protective finish. Let it dry for the allotted time suggested on your can. Once it is completely dry, you can dispose of your drop cloth or save it for your next project!

## STEP 12

Grab your hairpin legs and place one in each corner on the bottom of your TV stand. With a pencil, mark the holes where the screws will go. Remove the hairpin legs and predrill about ½" (1.3 cm) deep (not too deep; you don't want it coming out the other side!) for each hole. Place the hairpin legs back on the TV stand and secure with the included screws.

## STEP 13

Flip your new TV stand over and place it opposite your couch to give your living room a modern farmhouse touch that you'll love!

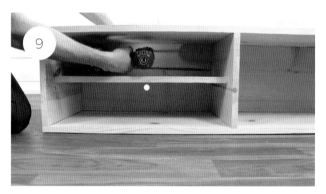

*Chapter 2*

# CLUTTER-FREE KITCHEN

The kitchen is the heart of the home and its natural gathering place. You could have the most spacious, beautiful living room, but host a party and you'll quickly notice everyone eventually makes their way into the kitchen. We kept this in mind when designing pieces for this chapter. We wanted to create functional organization as well as an inviting area for everybody to come together.

The biggest project in this chapter is the Oasis Kitchen Island (page 47). To keep this project suitable for beginners, we nixed the traditional cabinetry in favor of open storage. You still get the additional counter space and can store some fun, colorful accessories on the bottom. This adjustment makes it possible for this to be a one-day, easy DIY project. The towel bar gives it a little extra character and adds to the functionality. Once completed, you'll wonder how you ever lived without an island in your kitchen!

Another standout piece in this chapter is the Napa Valley Wine Rack (page 59). We designed this to store several bottles of wine, obvi, but we also decided to take it a step further with additional storage on top for your glassware, corkscrew and decanter. We round out the kitchen builds with a new barstool (page 53). Once you start building this, you'll realize that you need at least three more! Lucky for you, the simple design makes it a quick project.

*If you're in need of a little extra storage in your kitchen (and let's face it, who isn't?), then this easy project is calling your name. It's perfect for storing that cookbook that you're constantly referencing, your favorite coffee cups or the basil plant you've been struggling to keep alive. The piping on this shelf gives it an industrial look that is softened by the natural color. This project is quick and easy, requiring just one board and a few items from the plumbing section. Once you've knocked it out, you may just want to build a few more!*

# SHOWCASE SHELVING

DIMENSIONS: 30" W X 12¾" H X 11¼" D (76.2 CM X 32.4 CM X 28.6 CM)

LUMBER (WE USE STANDARD PINE)

1 X 12, 8' (2.4 m) long (x1)

Tape measure

Pencil

Safety glasses

Miter saw

Drill

2" (5.1-cm) trim-head screws

Screwdriver or impact driver

Wood filler

Sanding block or sander

Drop cloth

Rubber gloves

Brush

Polyurethane

4 (½" [1.3-cm]) black iron floor flanges

2 (½" x 10" [1.3 x 25.4-cm]) black steel pipe nipples

¾" (1.9-cm) wood screws

Stud finder

Level

Screws, for hanging

### STEP 1

Grab your tape measure and pencil and mark off the cuts of lumber you'll need for this project as described below. Make sure to put on your safety glasses and use your miter saw to make the necessary cuts. If you don't have a miter saw, many larger home improvement stores will cut the pieces for you.

Cut the 1 x 12 into three 30" (76.2-cm)-long pieces.

### STEP 2

Take one of your 1 x 12s and lay it flat on the ground. Take a second 1 x 12 and place it on edge so it's flush across the back of your first piece. It should look like a big, long, wooden "L."

### STEP 3

Predrill five evenly spaced holes through the second 1 x 12 into your first 1 x 12. Secure the pieces together with a trim-head screw in each predrilled hole.

### STEP 4

Take your third 1 x 12 and place one side flush across the top edge of your second 1 x 12. Now it should look like a big, long, wooden "C."

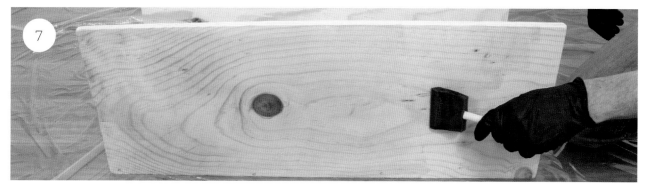

## STEP 5
Predrill another five holes, evenly spaced, this time through your third 1 x 12 into your second 1 x 12. Secure these pieces as well with your trim-head screws.

## STEP 6
Scoop out some wood filler with your fingertip and cover all of your screw holes. Once it dries, take your sanding block or sander to smooth out any rough edges and remove any excess wood filler.

## STEP 7
Lay out a drop cloth; it's time for polyurethane! Put on some rubber gloves and grab your brush. Cover your shelf with a coat of polyurethane, using smooth and even brush strokes. Watch out for drips! Let it dry for the allotted time suggested on your can. Once it is completely dry, you can dispose of your drop cloth or save it for your next project.

## STEP 8

Take your four floor flanges and screw one onto each end of your two pipes. It should look as if you have two mini-dumbbells.

## STEP 9

Lay out your shelf in the same way you originally assembled it: the first 1 x 12 is on the floor, the second 1 x 12 is vertical and the third 1 x 12 is on the top. Slide a mini-dumbbell into each outer corner in between your first and third 1 x 12s. Attach the mini-dumbbells to your shelf with a ¾" (1.9-cm) screw in each hole of the four floor flanges.

## STEP 10

Hanging this guy is easy! Use your stud finder to mark out two studs on your wall. Place your shelf against the wall spanning the two studs, with your level across the top. Once it's level, predrill two holes through your shelf into two studs in your wall. Secure the shelf to the wall, using screws long enough to reach the studs. Congrats, you're done! Your new shelf is all ready to display your finest kitchen wares.

*If your kitchen doesn't have an island, chances are you wish it did. Who wouldn't want that extra prep and seating space? Unfortunately, islands tend to be expensive to buy and have installed. This DIY version uses inexpensive pine boards and doesn't need to be attached to your floor, making it affordable and functional—if for some reason you need more space in your kitchen, it can be moved out or repositioned. It's large enough to become the centerpiece of your kitchen without overwhelming it. Since islands are a natural gathering place, you'll have plenty of opportunities to chat about how you made this one yourself!*

# OASIS KITCHEN ISLAND

DIMENSIONS: 48" L X 27¾" W X 36" H (1.2 M X 70.5 CM X 91.4 CM)

LUMBER (WE USE STANDARD PINE)

2 x 12, 8' (2.4 m) long (x1)

1 x 10, 12' (3.6 m) long (x1)

2 x 4, 8' (2.4 m) long (x2)

1 x 4, 8' (2.4 m) long (x2)

Tape measure

Pencil

Safety glasses

Miter saw

Drill

2" (5.1-cm) trim-head screws

Screwdriver or impact driver

Wood glue

Wood filler

Sanding block or sander

Drop cloth

Paintbrush and roller

Paint tray

Navy blue paint

1 (18" [45.7-cm]) towel bar

## STEP 1

Grab your tape measure and pencil and mark off the cuts of lumber you'll need for this project as described below. Make sure to put on your safety glasses and use your miter saw to make the necessary cuts. If you don't have a miter saw, many larger home improvement stores will cut the pieces for you.

Cut the 2 x 12 into two 45¾" (1.2-m)-long pieces.

Cut the 1 x 10 into three 48" (1.2-m)-long pieces.

Cut the 2 x 4s into four 35¼" (89.5-cm)-long pieces and two 22½" (57.2-cm)-long pieces.

Cut the 1 x 4s into two 47¼" (1.2-m)-long pieces and three 25½" (64.8-cm)-long pieces.

## STEP 2

Take your 1 x 4 pieces and lay them out in a figure eight pattern so that your three 25½" (64.8-cm) pieces are spread evenly between your two 47¼" (1.2-m) pieces. There should be 22½" (57.2 cm) of space between each 25½" (64.8-cm) piece.

## STEP 3

Predrill two holes about 2½" (6 cm) apart into each 47¼" (1.2-m) piece wherever it meets a 25½" (64.8-cm) piece (twelve holes total). Secure the figure eight framework together with a 2" (5.1-cm) trim-head screw in each predrilled hole.

## STEP 4

Spread a small bead of wood glue (about ⅛" [3 mm] wide) around the top edge of your framework. Be careful about putting too much on; you don't want it running down the sides.

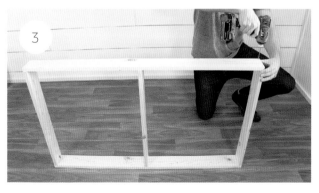

## STEP 5

Lay your three 1 x 10 pieces across the top of your framework so there is ³⁄₈" (1 cm) of overhang on each of the four sides.

## STEP 6

Predrill six holes (two at each end of the board and two in the middle) into each 1 x 10 where it matches up with the 1 x 4 framework underneath. Place a trim-head screw in each predrilled hole to secure the boards to your framework.

## STEP 7

Flip your framework over so the figure 8 side is facing up. Place a 35¼" (89.5-cm) piece of 2 x 4 in each corner. The 2" (5.1-cm) side of the 2 x 4 should line up with the 25½" (64.8-cm) side and the 4" (10.2-cm) side should line up with the 47¼" (1.2-m) side. These will be the legs of your island. Secure the legs to your framework by putting four trim-head screws through the framework into each leg (two on each side).

## STEP 8

Turn your island back over so it's standing upright. Take your two 22½" (57.2-cm) pieces of 2 x 4 and place them in between your island legs at each end. They should be placed 4" (10.2 cm) up from the ground. Secure these pieces to your island legs with your trim-head screws (four screws in each piece, two per side spaced about 2½" [6 cm] apart).

## STEP 9

Now lay your two 45¾" (1.2-m) pieces of 2 x 12 across the top of your 22½" (57.2-cm) crosspieces so that they're flush on each end. These will make a shelf for your island, giving you more of that ever-needed storage space. Predrill four holes into each board (two on each end) and secure to the crosspieces with your trim-head screws.

## STEP 10

Take your wood filler and apply, using your fingertip, to cover up any exposed screw holes. Once the wood filler is completely dry, use your sanding block or sander to eliminate any sharp edges, rough areas and excess wood filler.

## STEP 11

Woo-hoo, time for paint! Lay down a drop cloth and grab your brush and roller. Apply the navy blue paint until everything is completely covered. Let it dry completely. You may need to give it more than one coat to give it a smooth, finished look.

## STEP 12

Grab your towel bar and install it (per the instructions in the box) by centering it on one of the sides of your island. Move this baby into your kitchen.

*Is anyone else out there surprised by the price of bar stools? When you consider that you generally need to buy three or four, your kitchen upgrade budget can suddenly be wiped out before you've even started. We're here to help you save money with these simple and stylish barstools. The use of wood and pipe gives these stools an industrial feel, while the blue and gold soften the look and make them versatile enough to go from your kitchen island to the bar in your man cave.*

# BYO BARSTOOL

DIMENSIONS: 24" H X 16" W X 11¼" D (61 CM X 40.6 CM X 28.6 CM)

LUMBER (WE USE STANDARD PINE)

2 x 12, 6' (1.8 m) (x1)

Tape measure

Pencil

Safety glasses

Miter saw

Drill

2½" (6.4-cm) wood screws

Screwdriver or impact driver

Wood filler

Sanding block or sander

Drop cloth

Paintbrush

Navy blue paint

2 (¾" [7.6-cm]) steel floor flanges

1 (¾" x 12" [7.6 x 30.5-cm]) steel nipple pipe

Gold spray paint

1¼" (3.2-cm) wood screws

## STEP 1

Grab your tape measure and pencil and mark off the cuts of lumber you'll need for this project as described below. Make sure to put on your safety glasses and use your miter saw to make the necessary cuts. If you don't have a miter saw, many larger home improvement stores will cut the pieces for you.

Cut the 2 x 12 into two 22½" (57.2-cm)-long pieces and one 16" (40.6-cm)-long piece.

## STEP 2

Arrange your lumber in an upside-down "U" shape with the 22½" (57.2-cm) pieces making up the sides and the 16" (40.6-cm) piece on top.

## STEP 3

Predrill six holes (three on each side) through your 16" (40.6-cm) piece into your 22½" (57.2-cm) pieces. Secure your upside-down "U" together with a 2½" (6.4-cm) wood screw in each hole.

## STEP 4

Dab your finger into the wood filler and cover up the six screw holes. Once the wood filler has dried, take your sanding block or sander and smooth out your bar stool. Be sure to also remove any excess wood filler.

## STEP 5

It's time to show off your painting skills! Grab your drop cloth, paintbrush and navy blue paint and give your bar stool a fresh coat. You may need more than one coat to make sure your stool is completely covered.

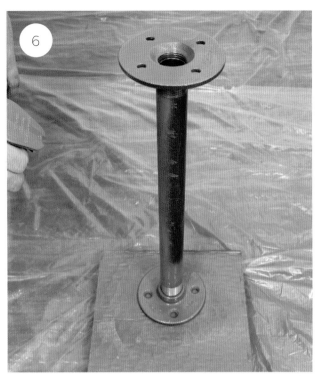

## STEP 6

While your bar stool is drying, take your floor flanges and screw one onto each end of your steel nipple pipe. Once everything is screwed together, spray it down with your gold spray paint (you may want to take your drop cloth and move this step outside). Make sure you don't overspray; you don't want the paint to get runny! Once everything is completely dry, you can dispose of your drop cloth or save it for your next project.

## STEP 7

Lay your barstool on its side. Slide your gold piping in between the sides of the stool. Place the piping so the floor flanges are 4" (10.2 cm) up from the bottom of the legs and toward the front. Secure the piping to your bar stool with a 1¼" (3.2-cm) wood screw in each of the floor flange holes. Stand the bar stool up and you're all done! Time to crack open a cold one and enjoy the fruits of your labor . . . or crack open 20 cold ones and fall off the fruits of your labor; either way works!

*Wine. Who doesn't love it? Well, JP doesn't love it, but he says toasting marshmallows instead of roasting marshmallows, so his opinion doesn't count. From the perfect food pairing to fueling a good girl's night, wine is as versatile as it is abundant. The United States produces hundreds of millions of gallons of wine each year! Given this info, it's likely that you have a few extra bottles (or six, in this case) on hand in your home. We have designed a perfect place to store them, as well as your glassware and decanter. Read on and get excited to display everything from your two-buck chuck to that extra special bottle you've been saving!*

# NAPA VALLEY WINE RACK

DIMENSIONS: 26¼" W X 11¼" H X 12" D (66.7 CM X 28.6 CM X 30.5 CM)

LUMBER (WE USE STANDARD PINE)

1 x 12, 8' (2.4 m) long (x1)

1 x 2, 4' (1.2 m) long (x1)

1 x 1, 3' (91.4 cm) long (x2)

Tape measure

Pencil

Safety glasses

Miter saw

Drill

1¼" (3.2-cm) trim-head screws

Screwdriver or impact driver

Wood filler (to match your stain color)

Sanding block or sander

Drop cloth

Rubber gloves

Rag

Stain

Brush

Polyurethane

Stud finder

Level

Screws, for hanging

## STEP 1

Grab your tape measure and pencil and mark off the cuts of lumber you'll need for this project as described below. Make sure to put on your safety glasses and use your miter saw to make the necessary cuts. If you don't have a miter saw, many larger home improvement stores will cut the pieces for you.

Cut the 1 x 12 into two 24¾" (62.9-cm)-long pieces, two 5" (12.7-cm)-long pieces and one 26¼" (66.7-cm)-long piece.

Cut the 1 x 2 into two 9¾" (24.8-cm)-long pieces and one 26¼" (66.7-cm)-long piece.

Cut the 1 x 1s into five 11¼" (28.6-cm)-long pieces.

## STEP 2

Take your five 11¼" (28.6-cm) pieces of 1 x 1 and space them evenly across one of your 24¾" (62.9-cm) pieces of 1 x 12. There should be 3½" (8.9 cm) of space on each end and 3½" (8.9 cm) of space in between each 1 x 1. Predrill two holes through each 1 x 1 into the 1 x 12 (one on each end of the 1 x 1), about 1" (2.5 cm) deep. Don't drill too deep; you don't want it coming out the other side. Secure the pieces together with a trim-head screw into each predrilled hole.

## STEP 3

Along with your 1 x 12 from Step 2, take your other 24¾" (62.9-cm) piece of 1 x 12 and two 5" (12.7-cm) pieces of 1 x 12 and arrange them in a rectangle. The 1 x 1s should be on the inside of the rectangle.

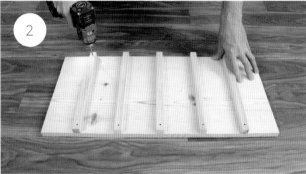

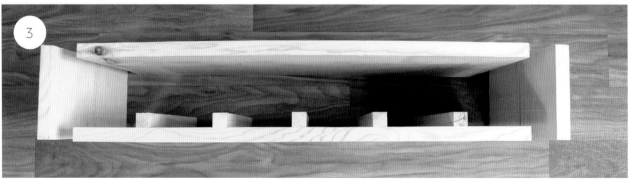

## STEP 4

Predrill three holes through the sides of each 5" (12.7-cm) piece into each 24¾" (62.9-cm) piece (one hole in the middle and one on each end for twelve holes total) and secure the rectangle together with a trim-head screw in each hole. Your rectangle should measure 26¼" x 5" (66.7 x 12.7 cm).

## STEP 5

Place your rectangle so the I x Is are on the bottom. Take your 26¼" (66.7-cm) piece of I x 12 and place it flush across the back.

## STEP 6

Predrill four evenly spaced holes through the 26¼" (66.7-cm) piece of I x 12 into each 24¾" (62.9-cm) piece of I x 12 (eight holes total). Secure the pieces together with a trim-head screw in each hole.

## STEP 7

Make a border around the top of your rectangle with the I x 2 pieces. Predrill four holes about 1" (2.5 cm) deep into the 26¼" (66.7-cm) piece of I x 2 and two into each 9¾" (24.8-cm) piece of I x 2. Secure the I x 2s with your trim-head screws.

## STEP 8

Dip your finger into the wood filler and cover all of the screw holes. Once dry, use your sanding block or sander to smooth any rough areas and remove any excess wood filler.

## STEP 9

Roll out a drop cloth and throw on some rubber gloves; it's staining time! Dip your rag and coat your wine rack with your favorite stain color. Once the stain dries, take your brush and give it a coat of polyurethane. Make sure to apply it evenly so you don't get any drips. Let it dry for the allotted time suggested on your can. Once it is completely dry, you can dispose of your drop cloth or save it for your next project.

## STEP 10

Time to hang this beauty! Using your stud finder, find your ideal wall placement and mark out two studs. Place your wine rack across the two studs with the level across the top. Once it's level, pre-drill two holes at the top of your wine rack that match up with the stud placement. Secure your wine rack to the wall with screws long enough to go through your holes and attach to the studs. Cheers, you're done!

# Chapter 3

# SIMPLY STYLISH DINING ROOM

Whether your dining room is formal or just a small corner of your living room, it deserves some love. After all, this is the space where friends and family come together to enjoy everything from frozen pizza and brewskies to full Thanksgiving dinners. You don't want to serve the turkey (or for our veggie friends out there like us: tofurkey) on a card table with some folding chairs, do you? The answer is no. No, you do not. You want your dining room to be more fancy than a frat house.

In this chapter, we're going to tackle three projects that will create a sophisticated and inviting space to dine and entertain. We'll start by showing you how to make the oh-so-important dining room table (page 67). This will be the centerpiece for your dining room and is finished with the stain color of your choice. This allows you to customize it to fit your personal taste. Hairpin legs give the rustic top a modern flair, so regardless of your light fixture, this table should fit in nicely. Once you've completed your dining room table, we'll move on to seating (page 73)! We've put together a set of simple instructions that will allow you to match the style of your dining table. Whether you build two benches for a more casual dining experience or choose to get a little more formal with a bench on one side and upholstered chairs on the other is completely up to you. This is what is so great about DIY—you are in control of the design!

Next up, we're going to build an accessory piece that is both unique and multi-functional. A sideboard (page 77) can be used for everything from a place to serve hors d'oeuvres to storage for dishes, linens and your secret stash of emergency whiskey. The hairpin legs on this piece keep the profile slim, making it perfect for dining rooms of all sizes. Once you've completed these builds, your final project will be planning a dinner party to show them all off!

*We've all seen big beautiful dining tables for sale at home stores. They are almost always accompanied by big, not-so-beautiful price tags. By using budget friendly pine boards and simple joinery techniques, we've seriously slashed the price tag on this statement piece of furniture without sacrificing beauty or functionality. This particular table features hairpin legs, a classic design element made popular in the mid-twentieth century. It's sure to impress anyone who has an appreciation for modern simplicity as well as all of your Mad Men loving friends. We love this piece because it's large enough for the whole family without a lot of added bulk, making it perfect for dining rooms of all sizes.*

# DINNER PARTY DINING TABLE

DIMENSIONS: 58" L X 38½" W X 30¼" H (1.5 M X 97.8 CM X 76.8 CM)

LUMBER (WE USE STANDARD PINE)

1 x 3, 8' (2.4 m) long (x2)

1 x 10, 10' (3 m) long (x2)

2 x 2, 10' (3 m) long (x1)

2 x 6, 10' (3 m) long (x1)

Tape measure

Pencil

Safety glasses

Miter saw

Drill

2" (5.1-cm) trim-head screws

Screwdriver or impact driver

Wood glue

Wood filler (to match your stain color)

Sanding block or sander

Drop cloth

Rubber gloves

Rag

Stain

Brush

Polyurethane

4 (28" [71.1-cm]) hairpin legs with included screws

### STEP 1

Grab your tape measure and pencil and mark off the cuts of lumber you'll need for this project as described below. Make sure to put on your safety glasses and use your miter saw to make the necessary cuts. If you don't have a miter saw, many larger home improvement stores will cut the pieces for you.

Cut the 1 x 3s into two 37" (94-cm)-long pieces and two 58" (1.5-m)-long pieces.

Cut the 1 x 10s into four 56½" (1.4-m)-long pieces.

Cut the 2 x 2 into two 56½" (1.4-m)-long pieces.

Cut the 2 x 6 into three 34" (86.4-cm)-long pieces.

### STEP 2

Arrange your two pieces of 2 x 2 side by side with enough room to place one 2 x 6 in between them at the top and another at the bottom. Place the last piece of 2 x 6 in the middle so the three 2 x 6s are evenly spaced; it should look like a giant "8".

### STEP 3

Predrill six holes down the side of each 2 x 2 so that two holes go into each 2 x 6. Secure this framework together using your 2" (5.1-cm) trim-head screws.

## STEP 4

Spread wood glue around your framework so it covers the top of your 2 x 2s and 2 x 6s. You don't need to glop it on, just a bead about ⅛" (3 mm) wide will do. Now take your four 1 x 10s and lay them flush across the top of your framework so that it's completely covered.

## STEP 5

Predrill four holes about 1½" (4 cm) deep in a square pattern through each 1 x 10 to match up with each of the three 2 x 6s underneath (twelve holes total). Predrill another six evenly spaced holes about 1½" (4 cm) deep down each 58" (1.5-m) side of your table into the the 2 x 2s underneath. Secure your 1 x 10s to the framework using your trim-head screws.

## STEP 6

Flip your tabletop over so the underside is facing up. Make a complete border around your tabletop with your 1 x 3s.

## STEP 7

Predrill six holes down each 57" (1.5-m) side border piece and four holes down each 37" (94-cm) end border piece, about 9" (23 cm) apart. Secure your border to the framework with your trim-head screws.

### STEP 8

Flip your table back over. Take your wood filler and apply, using your fingertip, to cover up any exposed screw holes. Once the wood filler is completely dry, use your sanding block or sander to eliminate any sharp edges, rough areas and excess wood filler. Make sure to sand the edges and corners so they're somewhat rounded; you don't want them cutting into your arms when you have your elbows up on the table.

### STEP 9

At last . . . stain! First, roll out a drop cloth to protect your floor. Put on your rubber gloves and dip your rag into the stain. Spread the stain evenly across your table and wipe away any excess. Once the stain is completely dry, apply a coat of polyurethane using your brush. Apply evenly and watch out for drips. You may want to add more than one coat for added protection and shine. Let it dry for the allotted time suggested on your can. Once it is completely dry, you can dispose of your drop cloth or save it for your next project.

### STEP 10

Place a 28" (71.1-cm) hairpin leg in each corner of the underside of your table top so that it fits up against your 1 x 3 border. Take a pencil and mark the holes where the screws will go. Remove the hairpin legs and predrill holes about 1" (2.5 cm) deep where you marked. Make sure you don't go too deep; you don't want to come out the other side. Put your hairpin legs back in place and secure them to your tabletop, using the hairpin leg screws.

### STEP 11

Flip this table over and center it under your dining room chandelier. Add some seating and you're ready for your next dinner party!

*Now that you have your dining room table, let's move on to seating! Bench seating is our favorite way to get the whole family around the dining table. It provides more versatility than chairs (the little ones can all pile onto one side) plus you can slide the bench under the table to free up space when not in use. We like to switch it up with a bench on one side and chairs on the other, but since this is DIY, your style is up to you!*

# MINIMALIST BENCH

DIMENSIONS: 48" L X 12¾" W X 17½" H (12 M X 32.4 CM X 44.5 CM)

LUMBER (WE USE STANDARD PINE)

1 x 2, 10' (3 m) long (x1)

2 x 12, 4' (1.2 m) long (x1)

Tape measure

Pencil

Safety glasses

Miter saw

Drill

2" (5.1-cm) trim-head screws

Screwdriver or impact driver

Wood filler (to match your stain color)

Sanding block or sander

Drop cloth

Rubber gloves

Rag

Stain

Brush

Polyurethane

4 (16" [40.6-cm]) hairpin legs with included screws

### STEP 1

Grab your tape measure and pencil and mark off the cuts of lumber you'll need for this project as described below. Make sure to put on your safety glasses and use your miter saw to make the necessary cuts. If you don't have a miter saw, many larger home improvement stores will cut the pieces for you.

Cut the 1 x 2 into two 48" (122-cm)-long pieces and two 11¼" (28.6-cm)-long pieces.

Cut the 2 x 12 into one 46½" (118.1-cm)-long piece.

### STEP 2

Start by making a complete border around your 46½" (118.1-cm) piece of 2 x 12 with your 1 x 2s. Predrill six holes about every 8" (20.5 cm) down the sides of the border and three on each end. Secure your 1 x 2 border to the 46½" (118.1-cm) piece of 2 x 12, using your 2" (5.1-cm) trim-head screws.

### STEP 3

Take your wood filler and apply, using your fingertip, to cover up any exposed screw holes. Once the wood filler is completely dry, use your sanding block or sander to eliminate any sharp edges, rough areas and excess wood filler. Make sure to sand the edges and corners so they're somewhat rounded; this will guarantee your bench will be comfortable to sit on.

## STEP 4

Time for that wonderful stain! Lay out your drop cloth and throw on some rubber gloves. Dip your rag into the stain and apply to your benchtop. Spread the stain evenly across your benchtop and wipe away any excess. Once the stain is dry, apply a coat of polyurethane using your brush. Apply evenly and watch out for drips. Let it dry for the allotted time suggested on your can. Once it is completely dry, you can dispose of your drop cloth or save it for your next project.

## STEP 5

Place a 16" (40.6-cm) hairpin leg in the underside of each corner of your benchtop so that it's just inside the 1 x 2 border. Take a pencil and mark the holes where the screws will go. Remove the hairpin legs and predrill holes about 1" (2.5 cm) deep in the areas you marked. Make sure you don't go too deep; you don't want to come out the other side. Put your hairpin legs back in place and secure them to your benchtop, using the hairpin leg screws.

## STEP 6

Flip this bench over and you're done. Slide it up next to that table you just built from the previous project and you have a perfect dining room set!

*Sideboards are perfect for entertaining: Serving food buffet style on a sideboard leaves room for large groups to eat at the dining table. We designed this particular sideboard to be simple and modern with separate storage compartments and hairpin legs. It's a quick build, using just two boards and a set of easy-to-attach hairpin legs, so if you are stressing out about where to put that cupcake bar for your sister's baby shower this weekend, we've got you covered!*

# SLEEK SIDEBOARD

DIMENSIONS: 48" W X 28¾" H X 11¼" D (1.2 M X 73 CM X 28.6 CM)

LUMBER (WE USE STANDARD PINE)

1 X 12, 8' (2.4 m) long (x2)

Tape measure

Pencil

Safety glasses

Miter saw

Drill

1½" (3.8-cm) trim-head screws

Screwdriver or impact driver

Wood filler (to match your stain color)

Sanding block or sander

Drop cloth

Rubber gloves

Rag

Stain

Brush

Polyurethane

4 (16" [40.6-cm]) hairpin legs with included screws

## STEP 1

Grab your tape measure and pencil and mark off the cuts of lumber you'll need for this project as described below. Make sure to put on your safety glasses and use your miter saw to make the necessary cuts. If you don't have a miter saw, many larger home improvement stores will cut the pieces for you.

Cut the 1 x 12s into three 48" (1.2-m)-long pieces and three 10½" (26.7-cm)-pieces.

## STEP 2

Place your three 10½" (26.7-cm) pieces on edge with 45¾" (1.2 m) of space between each. Take a 48" (1.2-m) piece and place it on edge along the top side of the 10½" (26.7-cm) pieces.

## STEP 3

Predrill two holes about 10" (25 cm) apart through the 48" (1.2-m) piece into each 10½" (26.7-cm) piece (six holes total). Secure the pieces together with a trim-head screw in each predrilled hole.

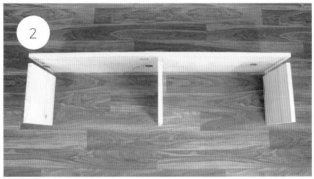

## STEP 4

Place another 48" (1.2-m) piece across the top of your framework. Predrill five evenly spaced holes along the backside of this piece into the edge of the 48" (1.2-m) piece underneath as well as one into the front edge of each 10½" (26.7-cm) piece (eight holes total). Secure the top piece with trim-head screws in each predrilled hole.

## STEP 5

Flip your framework over and repeat Step 4 with your third 48" (1.2-m) piece.

## STEP 6

Grab your wood filler and, using your fingertip, cover all of the exposed screw holes. Once it dries, use your sanding block or sander to smooth out any rough spots and remove any excess wood filler.

## STEP 7

Roll out your drop cloth and put on your rubber gloves. Dip your rag into your stain and apply it to your framework. Once the stain dries, use your brush to apply a coat of polyurethane. Let it dry for the allotted time suggested on your can. Once it is completely dry, you can dispose of your drop cloth or save it for your next project.

## STEP 8

Now, take your four hairpin legs and place one in each corner of the underside of your sideboard. With a pencil, mark where the screw holes will go. Remove the hairpin legs and predrill holes about ½" (1.3 cm) deep where you made the pencil marks. Don't drill too deep; you don't want to drill through the other side. Put the hairpin legs back onto your sideboard and attach them with the included screws.

## STEP 9

Flip this guy back onto its legs and you're all done! This piece will go great next to your dining room table so it's within an arm's reach of grabbing extra glasses, dishes, food and so forth!

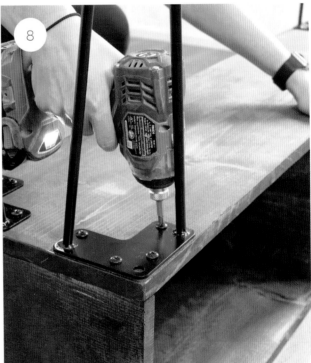

# Chapter 4

# BEDROOM OF YOUR DREAMS

Your bedroom is a space that should feel tranquil and serene. While it may be your escape from the rest of your home, you want the style to feel complementary.

We start this chapter out with the Dreamy Headboard (page 85). The bed is the centerpiece of this room and we want it to be beautiful! We used pine boards and chose a light-colored stain to show off the knots and grains in the wood. We gave it a frame for added dimension and to catch your head when you start dozing off early. We recommend keeping the bedding neutral to really let the wood shine! A bedroom isn't complete without a set of matching nightstands (page 91)! For these, we chose a simple open design with classic round tapered legs. This is one of the easier builds and a perfect complement to your new headboard. Together, they embody the modern farmhouse style that this book is all about: simple wood designs, with modern details that keep the look from getting too kitschy.

The next project is a sliding barn door (page 97)! This is an unexpected piece that packs a big punch with its emerald green color and unique pattern. It has a modern, smooth look and feel due to the MDF boards we used for both the backer and the diamond inserts. We guarantee that these three pieces will completely transform your bedroom!

*What do your college dorm room, your slacker ex-boyfriend's bedroom and that questionable hostel you stayed at in Amsterdam have in common? The answer: no headboard. You know why? A bedroom with a headboard says, "I've got my life together. I'm an adult. My parents no longer pay my bills, unless you include rent and my car payment." We're here to help you become the classy adult we know you are, with just a few pine boards and a can of stain. Who knew it could be so easy? While this project is physically bigger than most in this book, it is a straightforward design that only requires a few cuts and the same simple joinery techniques that you have come to expect. Get your miter saw ready; you're about to adult so hard.*

# DREAMY HEADBOARD

DIMENSIONS: 63½" W X 60¾" H
X 5½" D (1.6 M X 1.5 M X 14 CM)

LUMBER (WE USE STANDARD PINE)

2 x 4, 8' (2.4 m) long (x2)

1 x 12, 6' (1.8 m) long (x3)

1 x 6, 6' (1.8 m) long (x3)

| | | |
|---|---|---|
| Tape measure | Sanding block or sander |
| Pencil | Drop cloth |
| Safety glasses | Rubber gloves |
| Miter saw | Rag |
| Drill | Stain |
| 1½" (3.8-cm) trim-head screws | Brush |
| Screwdriver or impact driver | Polyurethane |
| Wood filler | |

### STEP 1

Grab your tape measure and pencil and mark off the cuts of lumber you'll need for this project as described below. Make sure to put on your safety glasses and use your miter saw to make the necessary cuts. If you don't have a miter saw, many larger home improvement stores will cut the pieces for you.

Cut the 2 x 4s into two 60" (1.5-m)-long pieces.

Cut the 1 x 12s into three 62" (1.6-m)-long pieces.

Cut the 1 x 6s into two 60" (1.5-cm)-long pieces and one 63½" (1.6-m)-long piece.

### STEP 2

Take your two 2 x 4s and space them 53" (1.3 m) apart.

### STEP 3

Place one of your 1 x 12s flush across the top of the 2 x 4s. Predrill three evenly spaced holes about 1½" (4 cm) deep through your 1 x 12 into each 2 x 4 (six holes total). Secure the 1 x 12 to your 2 x 4s with a trim-head screw in each predrilled hole.

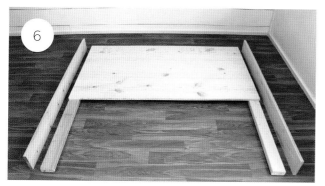

## STEP 4

Place a second 1 x 12 up against your first 1 x 12 and secure it to the 2 x 4s the same way you did in Step 3.

## STEP 5

One more time! Take your third 1 x 12, place it up against your second 1 x 12 and secure this one as you did in Steps 3 and 4.

## STEP 6

Lay your two 60" (1.5-m) pieces of 1 x 6 on edge so they match up with your 2 x 4s on either side of your headboard.

## STEP 7

Predrill five evenly spaced holes down the side of each 60" (1.5-m) piece of 1 x 6 so they match up with the 2 x 4s. Secure the 1 x 6s to the 2 x 4s with a trim-head screw in each predrilled hole.

## STEP 8

Place your 63½" (1.6-m) piece of 1 x 6 across the top of your headboard to match up with the 1 x 6 side pieces. Secure this piece at the ends with two trim-head screws in each 1 x 6 side piece. Secure in the middle portion with four trim-head screws evenly spaced through the 1 x 6 into the bordering 1 x 12. Make sure to predrill your holes first!

## STEP 9

Uncap your wood filler, dip your finger and cover all of your exposed screw holes. Once it dries, use your sanding block or sander to smooth out all of the rough edges and remove any excess wood filler.

## STEP 10

Lay out a drop cloth to protect your gorgeous floors, put on some rubber gloves and grab the stain. Dip your rag and rub a rich and luxurious coat on your headboard. Once the stain is dry, use your brush to apply a coat of polyurethane. Let it dry for the allotted time suggested on your can. Once it is completely dry, you can dispose of your drop cloth or save it for your next project. Stand your headboard up and you're finished! Doesn't it just make you want to snooze?

*We're suckers for modern furniture design. The clean lines, the fun legs, we love it all. We designed this simple nightstand to give off that modern feel, while still being functional. It's versatile enough to fit with any bedroom style, but we're partial to pairing it with the Dreamy Headboard. Because of its size and simple design, we recommend keeping the decor light—after all, the fewer distractions you have in your bedroom, the more relaxed you'll feel.*

# SNOOZE-BUTTON NIGHTSTAND

DIMENSIONS: 24¾" H X 18" W X 14½" D (62.9 CM X 45.7 CM X 36.8 CM)

LUMBER (WE USE STANDARD PINE)

1 x 8, 10' (3 m) long (x1)

Tape measure

Pencil

Safety glasses

Miter saw

Drill

1½" (3.8-cm) trim-head screws

Screwdriver or impact driver

Wood filler (to match your stain color)

Sanding block or sander

Drop cloth

Rubber gloves

Rag

Stain

Brush

Polyurethane

4 table leg straight-mounting T-plates with screws

4 (16" [40.6-cm]) round taper legs

### STEP 1

Grab your tape measure and pencil and mark off the cuts of lumber you'll need for this project as described below. Make sure to put on your safety glasses and use your miter saw to make the necessary cuts. If you don't have a miter saw, many larger home improvement stores will cut the pieces for you.

Cut the 1 x 8 into four 18" (45.7-cm)-long pieces, two 14½" (36.8-cm)-long pieces and one 16½" (41.9-cm)-long piece.

### STEP 2

Lay your 16½" (41.9-cm) piece on edge with a 14½" (36.8-cm) piece on either side to form a "U" shape.

### STEP 3

Predrill two holes through each 14½" (36.8-cm) piece into the 16½" (41.9-cm) piece at each corner. Secure the "U" framework together with a trim-head screw in each predrilled hole.

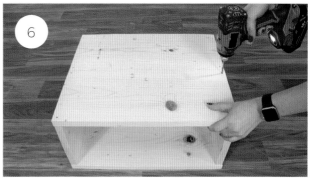

## STEP 4

Lay an 18" (45.7-cm) piece across the top so it's flush with the edges of your "U." Predrill seven holes total evenly spaced through the 18" (45.7-cm) piece into the "U" underneath, two into each 14½" (36.8-cm) piece and three into the 16½" (41.9-cm) piece. Secure the 18" (45.7-cm) piece with a trim-head screw in each predrilled hole.

## STEP 5

Take a second 18" (45.7-cm) piece and lay it flush against your first 18" (45.7-cm) piece. Predrill two holes at the corners on each side of the 18" (45.7-cm) piece into the 14½" (36.8-cm) pieces underneath. Secure the 18" (45.7-cm) piece with trim-head screws.

## STEP 6

Flip your nightstand over and repeat Steps 4 and 5 with your remaining two 18" (45.7-cm) pieces to complete the framework.

## STEP 7

Dip your fingertip into your wood filler and cover up any exposed screw holes. Once it dries completely, take your sanding block or sander to smooth out any rough spots and remove any excess wood filler.

## STEP 8

Unroll a drop cloth, put on some rubber gloves, dip your rag in the stain and apply a coat to your framework. Stain the round taper legs as well. Once the stain dries, take your brush and apply a coat of polyurethane. Let it dry for the allotted time suggested on your can. Once it is completely dry, you can dispose of your drop cloth or save it for your next project.

## STEP 9

Place a mounting T-plate into each corner on the underside of your framework and attach with the included screws. Now, all that's left to do is screw the four table legs into each mounting plate. Flip your nightstand onto its legs and you're all done! Place it next to your bed, add an alarm clock and you're all ready for the best sleep of your life.

*Barn doors are having a major moment. While we love a rustic farmhouse look as much as the next über-famous HGTV couple, we decided to give you a more modern, updated version. We kept it simple by using MDF boards for the entire project. The diamond design is classic and the emerald green paint gives it a fun, moody twist. You're just a few cuts and a coat of paint away from the standout feature of your bedroom. No room in your bedroom for a barn door? No problem! You can hang this piece anywhere in your home—from the office to a linen closet. The measurements given are for a standard door size and would cover an opening up to 36" (91.4 cm) wide.*

# MODERN-FARMHOUSE BARN DOOR

DIMENSIONS: 37" W X 79" H X 1½" D (94 CM X 2 M X 3.8 CM)

MDF BOARD (SHEETS)

4' x 8' x ¾" (1.2 m x 2.4 m x 1.9 cm) sheet (x1)

2' x 4' x ¾" (61 cm x 1.2 m x 1.9 cm) sheet (x1)

1" x 6" x 6' (2.5 x 15.2 x 1.8 m) board (x1)

1" x 2" x 8' (2.5 x 5.1 x 2.4 m) boards (x2)

Tape measure

Pencil

Safety glasses

Circular saw

Miter saw

Straight edge

Drill

1¼" (3.2-cm) trim-head screws

Screwdriver or impact driver

Wood filler

Sanding block or sander

Drop cloth

Paint tray

Emerald green paint

Paintbrush and roller

Barn Door Handle

Barn Door Track Hardware (6' [1.8 m])

## STEP 1

Grab your tape measure and pencil and mark off the cuts from the two MDF sheets you'll need for this project as described below. Make sure to put on your safety glasses and use your circular saw to make the necessary cuts. If you don't have a circular saw or miter saw for this project, many larger home improvement stores will cut the pieces for you.

Cut the 4' x 8' (1.2 x 2.4–m) sheet into one 37" x 79" (94-cm x 2-m) piece. This is the piece for the main door.

Cut the 2' x 4' (61-cm x 1.2-m) sheet in half so you have two 2' x 2' (61 x 61–cm) pieces.

Use your tape measure and pencil again and mark off the cuts from the MDF boards as described below. Make sure to put your safety glasses back on and use your miter saw to make the necessary cuts.

Cut the 1" x 6" x 6' (2.5 x 15.2 x 1.8–m) board into two 34" (86.4-cm)-long pieces.

Cut the 1" x 2" x 8' (2.5 x 5.1 x 2.4–m) boards into two 79" (2-m)-long pieces.

## STEP 2

Use your straight edge and pencil to make a line down the center of your door. The center point will be 18½" (47 cm) in from either side.

## STEP 3

Take one of your 79" (2-m) pieces of 1" x 2" (2.5 x 5–cm) MDF and place it flush down the right side of your 37" x 79" (94-cm x 2-m) sheet of MDF. Predrill seven holes evenly spaced about 1" (2.5 cm) deep running the length of your door through the 1" x 2" (2.5 x 5–cm) piece into the 37" x 79" (94-cm x 2-m) sheet underneath. Don't drill too deep; you don't want the holes coming through the other side. Secure the 1" x 2" (2.5 x 5–cm) piece with a trim-head screw in each predrilled hole.

## STEP 4

Now take a 1" x 6" (2.5 x 15–cm) piece and place it up against the 1" x 2" (2.5 x 5–cm) piece so it's flush with the top side of your door. Predrill eight holes about 1" (2.5 cm) deep in groups of two, evenly spaced, running the span of the 1" x 6" (2.5 x 15–cm) piece and into the 37" x 97" (94-cm x 2-m) sheet. Again, don't drill too deep. Secure the 1" x 6" (2.5 x 15–cm) piece with a trim-head screw in each predrilled hole.

## STEP 5

Time to attach those beautiful diamonds! Take one of your 2' x 2' (61 x 61–cm) squares, place it up against the 1" x 6" (2.5 x 15–cm) piece and line up two corners diagonally with your pencil line. The pencil line is a quick and easy way to make sure your diamonds are properly centered.

## STEP 6

Predrill five holes about 1" (2.5 cm) deep through your diamond and into the 37" x 79" (94-cm x 2-m) sheet, one in each corner and one in the center. Secure the diamond to your door with a trim-head screw in each predrilled hole.

## STEP 7

Two diamonds are better than one, right? Let's add a second one. Take your other 2' x 2' (61 x 61–cm) square, place a corner up against your first diamond and line it up diagonally with the pencil line as you did in Step 5. Attach it to your door the same way you did in Step 6.

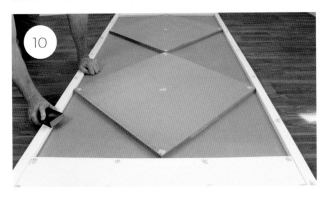

### STEP 8

Take your other 1" x 6" (2.5 x 15–cm) piece and place it up against your 1" x 2" (2.5 x 5–cm) piece so it's flush along the bottom side of your door. Attach it to your door the same way you did in Step 4.

### STEP 9

Place your other 1" x 2" (2.5 x 5–cm) piece flush against the left side of your door to complete the border. Attach it to your door the same way you did in Step 3.

### STEP 10

Bust out that wood filler, dip in your fingertip and cover all of the exposed screw holes across your door. Once it dries, take a sanding block or sander to remove any excess wood filler and smooth out any rough edges. MDF is smooth already, so the only rough edges should be along your cut lines.

### STEP 11

Roll out a drop cloth to avoid making a wonderful abstract painting on your floor. Uncap the emerald green paint and use your paintbrush and roller to cover your door. You may need more than one coat. Once it is completely dry, you can dispose of your drop cloth or save it for your next project! Attach a handle and track hardware of your choosing per the manufacturer's instructions and you're all done!

*When you think of a serving tray, you probably think of breakfast in bed. Although that scenario is always a welcome one, serving trays have so many other uses! They're perfect on a coffee table as a dedicated place to keep the remote controls. They look great on a kitchen island with flowers and a candle. They work well on a bathroom vanity to corral toiletries. This simple tray is so easy to make, you may find yourself making more to give away as gifts. Use the handles to customize it based on where you'll place it in your own home or tailor it to your gift recipient. If you're going for a modern feel, buy handles that have clean, straight lines. Use wrought iron, country-inspired handles for a more rustic, farmhouse look.*

# SIMPLE SERVING TRAY

DIMENSIONS: 24" L X 14½" W (61 CM X 36.8 CM)

LUMBER (WE USE STANDARD PINE)

1 x 8, 4' (1.2 m) long (x1)

1 x 2, 6' (1.8 m) long (x1)

Tape measure

Pencil

Safety glasses

Miter saw

Drill

1¼" (3.2-cm) trim-head screws

Screwdriver or impact driver

Wood filler (to match your stain color)

Sanding block or sander

Drop cloth

Rubber gloves

Rag

Stain

Brush

Polyurethane

2 front-mount handles with included screws

## STEP 1

Grab your tape measure and pencil and mark off the cuts of lumber you'll need for this project as described below. Make sure to put on your safety glasses and use your miter saw to make the necessary cuts. If you don't have a miter saw, many larger home improvement stores will cut the pieces for you.

Cut the 1 x 8 into two 24" (61-cm)-long pieces.

Cut the 1 x 2 into two 21" (53.3-cm)-long pieces and two 14½" (36.8-cm)-long pieces.

## STEP 2

Take your 1 x 2s and make a rectangle with the 14½" (36.8-cm) pieces on the sides and the 21" (53.3-cm) pieces in between them. The rectangle should measure 24" x 14½" (61 x 36.8 cm).

## STEP 3

Place a piece of 1 x 8 flush across the top of your rectangle on the backside. Predrill a total of seven holes about 1" (2.5 cm) deep through your 1 x 8 into the 1 x 2s underneath; two holes into each 14½" (36.8-cm) piece and three holes into the 21" (53.3-cm) piece all evenly spaced. Secure the 1 x 8 to your rectangle with a trim-head screw in each predrilled hole.

## STEP 4

Take your second piece of 1 x 8 and place it flush against your first piece of 1 x 8. Secure this piece to your rectangle in the same way you did in Step 3.

## STEP 5

Take your wood filler and use your fingertip to cover up the exposed screw holes. Once it dries, use your sanding block or sander to smooth out all of the rough edges and remove any excess wood filler.

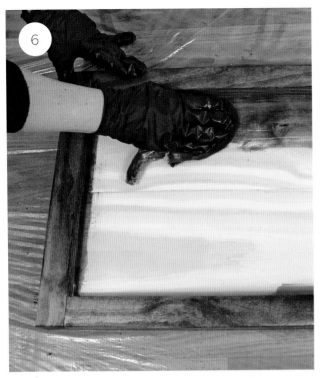

## STEP 6

Lay out a drop cloth and grab your rubber gloves; it's time to get staining! Dip in your rag and apply a coat to your serving tray. Once the stain dries completely, use your brush to apply a coat of polyurethane. Let it dry for the allotted time suggested on your can. Once it is completely dry, you can dispose of your drop cloth or save it for your next project.

## STEP 7

Lay your serving tray right side up. Center a handle on each of your 14½" (36.8-cm) pieces. Use the screws included with your handle to attach them to your serving tray. Your new tray is complete, well done!

*Chapter 5*

# WELCOME HOME ENTRYWAY

We have all been taught that first impressions matter. This applies to more than just your Tinder dates. An entryway is often one of the most overlooked areas of a home, especially when it is not the primary entrance for the owner. Not taking some time to make this area special is doing your home a real disservice. It is, after all, the first space that your guests see when they enter your home. Piled-up coats and shoes don't give off that welcoming vibe we all want to convey. In this chapter, we're showing you how to build two entryway basics: a coat rack (page 111) and a shoe rack (page 117). These pieces are an absolute must if you don't have an entryway closet, but also come in handy if you do, to keep your frequently used shoes and jackets more accessible. We designed these pieces as a matching pair, both made out of wood and painted black, to give your entryway a simple and cohesive look.

We've also included a console table (page 123) in this chapter. This is a simple project that will bring some much needed convenience into your life. The narrow, tapered legs keep the project slim, perfect for entryways of any size. Whether you decide to place it directly in your entryway or farther into your home, you'll fall in love with this superfunctional piece!

*We love an organized home entry. As any parent can attest, it makes getting in and out the door so much faster. Having a coat rack can really help to streamline this process. We designed this piece with large hooks that allow you to quickly grab or hang a jacket or purse. Not having to fumble with hangers or small pegs is a serious time saver. We also added storage to house your keys, dog bags, sunglasses and those reusable grocery bags that make you feel superior to everyone else in line at Trader Joe's. This build is fun, quick and easy!*

# ENTRYWAY COAT RACK

DIMENSIONS: 36" W X 11¼" H X 6" D (91.4 CM X 28.6 CM X 15.2 CM)

LUMBER (WE USE STANDARD PINE)

1 x 12, 3' (91.4 cm) long (x1)

1 x 6, 8' (2.4 m) long (x1)

Tape measure

Pencil

Safety glasses

Miter saw

Drill

1½" (3.8-cm) trim-head screws

Screwdriver or impact driver

Wood filler

Sanding block or sander

Drop cloth

Paintbrush and roller

Black paint

4 coat hooks with included screws

Stud finder

Level

Screws, for hanging

### STEP 1

Grab your tape measure and pencil and mark off the cuts of lumber you'll need for this project as described below. Make sure to put on your safety glasses and use your miter saw to make the necessary cuts. If you don't have a miter saw, many larger home improvement stores will cut the pieces for you.

Cut the 1 x 6s into two 36" (91.4-cm)-long pieces and two 4½" (11.4-cm)-long pieces.

Your 1 x 12 is already the correct length—yay!

### STEP 2

Take your 1 x 6 pieces and arrange them on their edges into a rectangle. The 4½" (11.4-cm) pieces should be in between the 36" (91.4-cm) pieces.

### STEP 3

Predrill a total of eight holes, two at each joint. Secure your rectangle with a trim-head screw in each predrilled hole.

## STEP 4

With your rectangle on end, place your 36" (91.4-cm) piece of 1 x 12 across the top so it's flush down one side.

## STEP 5

Predrill ten holes through your 1 x 12 where it matches up with your rectangle (five holes evenly spaced into each 36" [91.4-cm] length of the rectangle). Secure your 1 x 12 to the rectangle with your trim-head screws.

## STEP 6

Take your wood filler and, using your fingertip, cover up your screw holes. Once it dries, use your sanding block to smooth out any rough edges and remove any excess wood filler.

## STEP 7

Time to make this coat rack look a little more finished! Lay out a drop cloth and grab your paintbrush. Give your coat rack the once-over with your black paint. If that doesn't cover everything, you may need to give it a second coat. Once it is completely dry, you can dispose of your drop cloth or save it for your next project.

## STEP 8

Let's finish this guy up! Space your four coat hooks evenly across your coat rack. With the included screws, secure the hooks in place.

## STEP 9

Your new coat rack will look so much better if it's hung on a wall, so let's do that. Using your stud finder, mark the placement of two studs in the wall where you'll be putting your coat rack. Place your coat rack level against the wall across the two studs, with the level on top. Once it's level, predrill two holes inside your rectangle going through the coat rack and into the studs. Secure it to the wall using screws long enough to reach to the studs. You're all done—nice work!

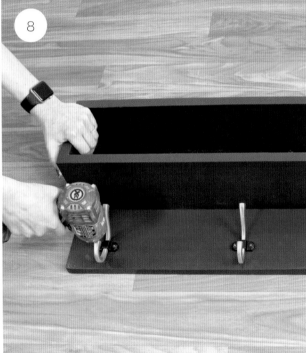

*Nothing makes an entryway look messier than shoes strewn all over the place. We want to create a welcome space for you and your guests, so let's tidy things up a bit, shall we? We created this shoe rack with smaller entryways in mind. The multilevel design saves space without sacrificing function. We painted it to match the coat rack and give your entry a cohesive feel. We designed them as a matching pair, but it's small enough to fit in a closet if you're going for that minimalist vibe.*

# SHOE ADDICT RACK

DIMENSIONS: 36" W X 20" H X 14¼" D (91.4 CM X 50.8 CM X 36.2 CM)

LUMBER (WE USE STANDARD PINE)

1 X 12, 6' (1.8 m) long (x1)

2 X 2, 8' (2.4 m) long (x2)

Tape measure

Pencil

Safety glasses

Miter saw

Drill

2" (5.1-cm) trim-head screws

Screwdriver or impact driver

Wood filler

Sanding block or sander

Drop cloth

Paintbrush

Black paint

Rubber gloves

Brush

Polyurethane

2" (5-cm) black screws

### STEP 1

Grab your tape measure and pencil and mark off the cuts of lumber you'll need for this project as described below. Make sure to put on your safety glasses and use your miter saw to make the necessary cuts. If you don't have a miter saw, many larger home improvement stores will cut the pieces for you.

Cut the 1 x 12 into two 36" (91.4-cm)-long pieces.

Cut the 2 x 2s into four 20" (50.8-cm)-long pieces and six 11¼" (28.6-cm)-long pieces.

### STEP 2

Take two 20" (50.8-cm) pieces of 2 x 2, lay them side by side and place an 11¼" (28.6-cm) piece of 2 x 2 as a crosspiece in between them so you have a "U" shape. Predrill two holes through each 20" (50.8-cm) piece and into your 11¼" (28.6-cm) piece. Secure the "U" together with trim-head screws in each predrilled hole.

### STEP 3

Working from the bottom of your "U," place another 11¼" (28.6-cm) piece of 2 x 2 so there are 3¾" (9.5 cm) of space between the two crosspieces. Secure by predrilling and screwing as you did for the first crosspiece in Step 2.

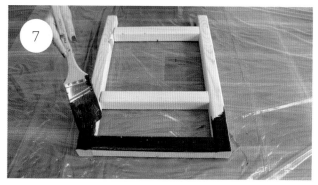

## STEP 4

Place your third 11¼" (28.6-cm) crosspiece 10¾" (27.3 cm) up from your second crosspiece. Secure this as well, as you did for your first two crosspieces in Steps 2 and 3.

## STEP 5

That was fun, right? So much fun, in fact, that you get to do it all over again! Repeat Steps 2 through 4 so you have two sets of 2 x 2 framework.

## STEP 6

Dip your finger into your wood filler and plug up all of your screw holes. Once it dries, sand off any sharp edges or extra wood filler from your framework.

## STEP 7

Time for paint! Lay out a drop cloth and grab that black paint and paintbrush. Apply a coat so your framework is completely covered. You may need to apply a second coat for a smooth, finished look.

## STEP 8

While the paint is drying, put on your rubber gloves and grab your polyurethane and brush. Apply a coat to each of your pieces of 1 x 12. Make sure to watch out for dripping! Let it dry for the allotted time suggested on your can. Once everything is completely dry, you can dispose of your drop cloth or save it for your next project!

## STEP 9

Place your black framework on their edges, about 31" (78 cm) apart. Take a 1 x 12 and thread it between your first and second crosspieces so it rests against your second crosspiece. There should be 1" (2.5 cm) of overhang on each side. Predrill two holes 2" (5.1 cm) deep into each crosspiece. Make sure not to go too deep; you don't want it coming out of the 1 x 12. Secure them together with two black screws through each crosspiece into the 1 x 12.

## STEP 10

Take your other 1 x 12 and place it between your second and third crosspieces so it rests against your third crosspiece. Make sure there is 1" (2.5 cm) of overhang on each side as well and secure this together the same way you did in Step 9.

## STEP 11

Stand your rack on its feet. Predrill a total of eight more holes, one where each 2 x 2 meets up with the edges of your 1 x 12s (front and back). Secure a black screw into each hole. You're all done, time to show off your best shoes!

*The console table is one of the most versatile pieces of furniture out there! Need a landing spot for your keys? Console table. A place for your lamp? Console table. What about the framed photos of all these nieces and nephews? The answer is always the console table. We designed this piece to be modern and functional. The tapered legs gave us the modern look we wanted. For functionality, we created storage in the center as well as separated storage on each end. This step doesn't add any more difficulty; we're still making straight cuts with common tools, but it creates a unique look that'll stand out.*

# DOUBLE-DUTY CONSOLE TABLE

DIMENSIONS: 48" W X 28¾" H X 11¼" D (1.2 M X 73 CM X 28.6 CM)

LUMBER (WE USE STANDARD PINE)

1 X 12, 8' (2.4 M) long (x2)

Tape measure

Pencil

Safety glasses

Miter saw

Drill

1¼" (3.2-cm) trim-head screws

Screwdriver or impact driver

Wood filler

Sanding block or sander

Drop cloth

Paint tray

Black paint

Paintbrush and roller

Rubber gloves

Rag

Stain

4 table leg angled mounting T-plates with screws

4 (16" [40.6-cm]) round taper legs

## STEP 1

Grab your tape measure and pencil and mark off the cuts of lumber you'll need for this project as described below. Make sure to put on your safety glasses and use your miter saw to make the necessary cuts. If you don't have a miter saw, many larger home improvement stores will cut the pieces for you.

Cut your 1 x 12s into three 48" (1.2-m)-long pieces, two 9¾" (24.8-cm)-long pieces and two 9" (22.9-cm)-long pieces.

## STEP 2

Take your two 9¾" (24.8-cm) pieces and put them on edge up against the side of one of your 48" (1.2-m) pieces. Place them so that each one is 8¼" (21 cm) away from an end of the 48" (1.2-m) piece.

## STEP 3

Predrill two holes through your 48" (1.2-m) piece into each 9¾" (24.8-cm) piece (four holes total). Secure them together with a trim-head screw in each predrilled hole.

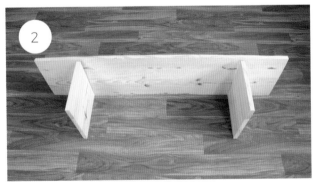

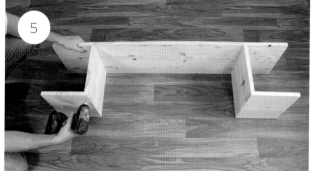

### STEP 4

Now take your two 9" (22.9-cm) pieces and place one of the ends on each of the front edges of the 9¾" (24.8-cm) pieces. These will make the cubbies that give the "Double-Duty Console Table" its world-famous name.

### STEP 5

Predrill two holes through each 9" (22.9-cm) piece into each 9¾" (24.8-cm) piece (four holes total). Secure them together with a trim-head screw in each predrilled hole.

### STEP 6

Take another 48" (1.2-m) piece and place it flush across the top of your framework. The edges of the 48" (1.2-m) piece should match up with the edges of your framework.

## STEP 7

Predrill holes across your top 48" (1.2-m) piece so they match up with your framework underneath. There should be two holes drilled into each 9¾" (24.8-cm) piece, two holes into each 9" (22.9-cm) piece and five holes, evenly spaced, into the 48" (1.2-m) piece underneath. Secure this together with your trim-head screws in each predrilled hole.

## STEP 8

Flip your table over and repeat Steps 6 and 7 with your other 48" (1.2-m) piece.

## STEP 9

Crack open your wood filler, dip in your finger and plug all of your screw holes with the wood filler. Once it dries, take your sanding block or sander and smooth out any rough edges and remove any excess wood filler.

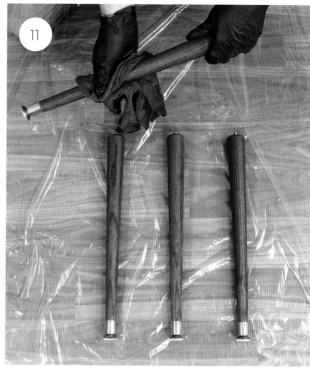

## STEP 10

Lay down a drop cloth and grab your brush, it's time to paint! Pour out some black paint into your paint tray and use your roller to give your table a nice coat. Use your paintbrush to reach any corners or cracks your roller can't reach. You may need to give it more than one coat for an even look.

## STEP 11

While the paint is drying, put on your rubber gloves and uncap your stain. Dip in your rag and cover each of your round taper legs. This is going to give some great contrast between the stained legs and the painted framework. Once everything is dry, you can dispose of your drop cloth or save it for your next project.

## STEP 12

Take your four table leg angled mounting T-plates and put one in each corner, 3" (7.6 cm) away from the ends on the bottom of your console table. Secure the T-plates to your console table with the included screws.

## STEP 13

Take your four round taper legs and screw one tightly into each mounting T-plate.

## STEP 14

All that's left is to flip it back over onto its legs and decide what you're going to do with those side cubbies. You might wanna just stick a couple of succulents in there and call it a day.

# Chapter 6

# SANCTUARY BATHROOM

Would you describe your bathroom as spalike? Beautiful? Tranquil? Not many people would, but we are here to help you say just that. Since bathrooms tend to be some of the smaller rooms in the house, just a few small additions can have a big impact. This chapter focuses on those small details that will add tons of charm to your bathroom.

Our first project is an upgraded mirror (page 133). We'll start with pine boards to create a frame and ledge and then add a frameless mirror to the inside. The result is a custom piece that looks way more expensive than it actually is! After the mirror, we'll tackle the towel bar (page 139). We made this one extra-wide so you can go ahead and splurge on those big fluffy towels for your newly improved bathroom. We designed this with clean lines and gave it extra coats of polyurethane to help protect the stain finish.

Finally, we created a custom shelf (page 145) to sit across your bathtub. It is designed to hold all your bath essentials, including a glass of wine! Once you make one of these for yourself, you will realize that it makes a perfect gift for the master relaxer in your life. You know who we're talking about: the person who spends full nights soaking away their worries with bath bombs and mud masks. Go ahead and make this for them! You can thank us later!

*We love the look of a wood-framed mirror, but they can be so expensive! As it turns out, this is an easy project that offers more practicality than a traditional framed mirror. This version features a shelf where you can display everything from your hipster beard oil to your favorite razor. For this project you'll be purchasing a frameless mirror. They're cheap and easy to find online or in hardware stores. You'll frame it out with some simple pine boards and add a ledge. Once you're done, take a step back and admire your work and your sweat-free complexion!*

# UPGRADE-YOUR-LOOK MIRROR

DIMENSIONS: 27¼" W X 34" H X 5½" D (69.2 CM X 86.4 CM X 14 CM)

LUMBER (WE USE STANDARD PINE)

1 x 3, 10' (3 m) long (x1)

1 x 2, 10' (3 m) long (x1)

1 x 6, 3' (91.4 cm) long (x1)

Tape measure

Pencil

Safety glasses

Miter saw

Drill

1¼" (3.2-cm) trim-head screws

Screwdriver or impact driver

Sanding block or sander

Drop cloth

Rubber gloves

Rag

Stain

Brush

Polyurethane

2 D-ring picture hanging hooks with screws

Superglue

1 (24" x 30" [61 x 76.2-cm]) frameless mirror

Level

Wall anchors with screws

### STEP 1

Grab your tape measure and pencil and mark off the cuts of lumber you'll need for this project as described below. Make sure to put on your safety glasses and use your miter saw to make the necessary cuts. If you don't have a miter saw, many larger home improvement stores will cut the pieces for you.

Cut your 1 x 3 into two 33¼" (84.5-cm)-long pieces and two 22¼" (56.5-cm)-long pieces.

Cut your 1 x 2 into two 30¼" (76.8-cm)-long pieces and two 27¼" (69.2-cm)-long pieces.

Cut your 1 x 6 into one 27¼" (69.2-cm)-long piece.

### STEP 2

Take your 1 x 3 pieces and arrange them into a rectangle with the 22¼" (56.5-cm) pieces on the top and bottom and the 33¼" (84.5-cm) pieces running the full length of the sides.

### STEP 3

Make another rectangle on top of your first one with your 1 x 2 pieces. Place the 27¼" (69.2-cm) pieces on the top and bottom and the 30¼" (76.8-cm) pieces on the sides, so the 1 x 2 rectangle matches up with the outside border of the 1 x 3 rectangle. Work your way around the border, predrilling holes about 1" (2.5 cm) deep through your 1 x 2s into your 1 x 3s underneath. Don't drill too deep; you don't want them going through the other side of your 1 x 3s. Make sure to predrill three holes into each corner of your 1 x 2 top and bottom pieces; two going into your 1 x 3 side pieces underneath and one going into each of your 1 x 3 top and bottom pieces underneath. Secure the two rectangles together with a trim-head screw in each predrilled hole.

## STEP 4

Time to add a helpful little shelf to your mirror! Take your 27¼" (69.2-cm) piece of 1 x 6 and lay it flush across the edge of your mirror frame. There should be 4" (10.2 cm) of overhang on the side of your mirror with the 1 x 3s.

## STEP 5

Predrill four holes, evenly spaced, through your 1 x 6 into your mirror frame and secure with trim-head screws.

## STEP 6

Use your sanding block or sander to remove any rough edges or areas of your mirror frame.

## STEP 7

Roll out a drop cloth and put on some rubber gloves. Crack open that beautiful stain and dip in your rag. Give your mirror a nice even coat, making sure to wipe away any excess. Once the stain is dry, take your brush and give your mirror a coat of polyurethane. Let it dry for the allotted time suggested on your can. Once it is completely dry, you can dispose of your drop cloth or save it for your next project.

### STEP 8

Take your two D-ring picture hanging hooks and place one in the top of each corner on the backside of your mirror frame. Secure the hooks to your mirror frame with the included screws.

### STEP 9

Finally, the mirror part! Let's face it, without the mirror, you've just spent the better part of your day making a useless wooden rectangle. Start by placing a bead of superglue about $\frac{1}{8}$" (3 mm) wide around the inside track on the back of your mirror. You don't need a ton; superglue expands and you don't want it creeping out onto the exposed part of your mirror!

### STEP 10

Lay your mirror (shiny side down!) into the track over the superglue. Press down firmly so the mirror matches up with the glue. Let the superglue dry completely in accordance to the recommendations on the bottle.

### STEP 11

Time to hang this beauty! Use your level to make two level marks on your wall that match up with the amount of space in between your hooks. Drill two holes into the marked areas and insert a wall anchor and corresponding screw into each. Hang your mirror onto the screws from the hooks. You're all done!

*When we set out to design a towel bar, we had a few important criteria. First, it had to be functional and to us that meant wide enough to hold multiple towels. No one wants one towel on the bar and another hanging over the shower door—that really throws off the whole relaxing spa vibe we're going for. After functional, we wanted it to look great! We settled on clean lines and a light tone that would let the wood shine through. This is a quick and easy DIY that'll bring timeless style to the only room where you can hide out from your kids!*

# MODERN TOWEL BAR

DIMENSIONS: 36" W X 6¼" H X 3½" D (91.4 CM X 15.9 CM X 8.9 CM)

LUMBER (WE USE STANDARD PINE)

1 x 3, 4' (1.2 m) long (x1)

1 x 4, 3' (91.4 cm) long (x1)

1 x 6, 3' (91.4 cm) long (x1)

Tape measure

Pencil

Safety glasses

Miter saw

Drill

1¼" (3.2-cm) trim-head screws

Screwdriver or impact driver

Wood filler (to match your stain color)

Sanding block or sander

Drop cloth

Rubber gloves

Rag

Stain

Brush

Polyurethane

Stud finder

Level

Screws, for hanging

## STEP 1

Grab your tape measure and pencil and mark off the cuts of lumber you'll need for this project as described below. Make sure to put on your safety glasses and use your miter saw to make the necessary cuts. If you don't have a miter saw, many larger home improvement stores will cut the pieces for you.

Cut the 1 x 3 into one 36" (91.4-cm)-long piece and two 2" (5.1-cm)-long pieces.

Hooray! Your 1 x 4 and 1 x 6 are already the right size, so you don't need to cut them.

## STEP 2

Take your two 2" (5.1-cm) pieces of 1 x 3 and stand them on end 36" (91.4 cm) apart. Place your 36" (91.4-cm) piece of 1 x 3 flush across the top of these two pieces.

## STEP 3

Predrill four holes (two on each end) through the 36" (91.4-cm) piece into the 2" (5.1-cm) pieces. Secure them together with a trim-head screw in each predrilled hole.

### STEP 4

Flip it over so it looks like a big, elongated "U." Take your 1 x 6 and place it over the "U" so that it's flush down one side.

### STEP 5

Predrill four holes (two on each end) through your 1 x 6 piece into the 2" (5.1-cm) pieces. Secure them together with your trim-head screws.

### STEP 6

Flip this guy up so the 1 x 6 is on edge. Take your 36" (91.4-cm) piece of 1 x 4 and place it across the top edge of your 1 x 6. Predrill five holes, evenly spaced, along the top edge and secure together with your trim-head screws.

## STEP 7

Bust out that wood filler, dip in your finger and cover up all of the exposed screw holes. Once the wood filler is dry, take your sander or sanding block to smooth out any rough spots and remove any excess wood filler.

## STEP 8

Uncap that favorite stain of yours, break out that rag and give your towel rack a coat of luxurious color. Be sure to put down a drop cloth and wear rubber gloves!

## STEP 9

Once the stain is dry, give your towel rack at least three coats of polyurethane, using your brush. The additional coats of polyurethane will provide extra protection against moisture from all of those wet towels. Let it dry for the allotted time suggested on your can. Once it is completely dry, you can dispose of your drop cloth or save it for your next project.

## STEP 10

To hang your new towel rack, use your stud finder to mark off two studs. Place your towel bar against the wall across the two studs with the level on top. Once the towel bar is level, predrill two holes through your 1 x 6 so they match up with two studs in your wall. Secure your rack to the wall with screws long enough to reach your studs. You're all done; go ahead and hang up your favorite bath towel!

*What does the ultimate night of relaxation look like to you? If it involves a bath, a book and a glass of wine, then you, my friend, have turned to the right page! We've made it easy for you to combine all three without having to fear wet pages or the accident waiting to happen when you combine glassware and a slippery tub ledge. For this tutorial, we created a flat surface for candles, body oil or your favorite sub sandwich (don't worry, we won't judge). Next, we added two ledges to hold up that book you can't put down. To ensure that your glass of Cabernet doesn't spill and create a horror scene in your tub, we added a perfect wineglass-sized cutout. Break out your tools, because you have the ultimate reward waiting for you at the end of this project!*

# WINE-AND-CANDLES TUB SHELF

DIMENSIONS: 30" W X 4" H X 11¼" D (76.2 CM X 10.2 CM X 28.6 CM)

LUMBER (WE USE STANDARD PINE)

1 x 12, 3' (91.4 cm) long (x1)

1 x 3, 3' (91.4 cm) long (x1)

1 x 1, 3' (91.4 cm) long (x1)

Tape measure

Pencil

Safety glasses

Miter saw

Drill

1¼" (3.2-cm) trim-head screws

Screwdriver or impact driver

Wine glass

Jigsaw

Wood filler (to match your stain color)

Sanding block or sander

Drop cloth

Rubber gloves

Rag

Stain

Brush

Polyurethane

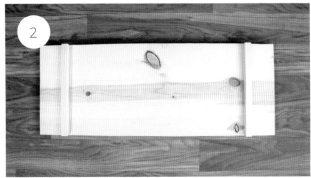

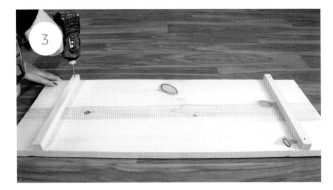

## STEP 1

Grab your tape measure and pencil and mark off the cuts of lumber you'll need for this project as described below. Make sure to put on your safety glasses and use your miter saw to make the necessary cuts. If you don't have a miter saw, many larger home improvement stores will cut the pieces for you.

Cut the 1 x 12 into one 30" (76.2-cm)-long piece.

Cut the 1 x 3 into one 30" (76.2-cm)-long piece.

Cut the 1 x 1 into one 12" (30.5-cm)-long piece and two 11¼" (28.6 cm) pieces.

## STEP 2

Measure the distance between the inside edges of your bathtub where you'll be placing your tub shelf. Take that measurement and subtract 2" (5.1 cm). For example, if the distance between the inside edges of your bathtub is 24" (61 cm), your measurement will be 22" (55.9 cm). Lay out your 30" (76.2-cm) piece of 1 x 12 and place your two 11¼" (28.6 cm) pieces of 1 x 1 across the top so they are the same distance apart from each other as your bathtub measurement. In keeping with our example, we would place them 22" (55.9 cm) apart from each other.

## STEP 3

Predrill two holes about 1" (2.5 cm) deep through each 1 x 1 into the 1 x 12. Don't drill too deep; you don't want your holes coming out the other side of the 1 x 12. Secure both 1 x 1s to your 1 x 12 with a trim-head screw in each predrilled hole.

## STEP 4

Flip your shelf over onto the other side. Take the smallest wineglass you have and trace a circle onto your shelf, using the lip of your glass as a guide. Your circle should be centered about 3" (7.6 cm) in from the front side of your shelf and just on the inside of the 1 x 1 underneath the right side. (You can also trace it on the left side instead, if you're a lefty!)

## STEP 5

Take your other 1 x 1 and use it as a guide to trace a channel from your circle to the front side of your shelf.

## STEP 6

Use your jigsaw to cut out the channel and circle on your shelf. This will be your trusty wineglass holder, a must have for any tub shelf!

## STEP 7

Now take your 30" (76.2-cm) piece of 1 x 3 and place it on edge on the back of your shelf. Predrill four evenly spaced holes from the underside of your shelf into the 1 x 3. Attach the 1 x 3 to your shelf with a trim-head screw in each predrilled hole.

## STEP 8

Take your 12" (30.5-cm) piece of 1 x 1 and center it on your shelf so it's 2" (5.1 cm) in front of your 1 x 3. Predrill a hole about 1" (2.5 cm) deep through each end of your 1 x 1 (again, don't drill too deep) and secure it to your shelf with trim-head screws. This, along with your 1 x 3, will act as a little holder for your tablet, phone, books or anything else you care to look at while you bathe yourself into a nirvana-like state of relaxation.

## STEP 9

Using your fingertip and wood filler, fill all of your exposed screw holes except for the screw holes of the 11¼" (28.6-cm) piece of 1 x 1 underneath your shelf. You'll want to leave those exposed in case you need to do any adjusting of their placement in the future. Once the wood filler is dry, take your sander or sanding block to smooth out any rough spots and remove any excess wood filler.

## STEP 10

Lay down a drop cloth and throw on some rubber gloves; you've got some staining to do! Apply a coat to your shelf with your rag, using smooth and even strokes. Once the stain dries, use your brush to apply the polyurethane. You'll want extra protection with the shelf being in a wet environment, so two or three coats is ideal. Let it dry for the allotted time suggested on your can. Once it is completely dry, you can dispose of your drop cloth or save it for your next project. Your new tub shelf is all done—time to hop in the tub with a good book and a glass of wine!

# ACKNOWLEDGMENTS

First off, we would like to thank everyone who has followed The Rehab Life on YouTube, Facebook and Instagram over these last few years. Without you, this book would not have happened. Your support keeps us motivated to continue creating approachable DIY projects for everyone. It's the greatest feeling in the world when we receive pictures of the builds you have made from our tutorials. For this, we thank you!

We would also like to thank all of our family and friends. We may have had some crazy ideas and taken a less-than-sure-thing career path, but you have always supported our choices. No one gets to where they are alone, so thank you for your guidance and helping us to grow into what we are today.

Last, but certainly not least, a big shout out to the star of our YouTube videos, the little shelter dog known as Henry (or Henderson if we're at a formal gathering). He brings a little extra ray of sunshine to each day and makes our photo and video shoots that much more enjoyable. We're guessing he may have something to do with the number of followers we have.

# ABOUT THE AUTHORS

JP and Liz met as servers at Outback Steakhouse in Roseville, Minnesota (shout out to the mashed potato sandwich). JP trained Liz on her first day, but by the end of their shift, she was telling him what to do. Aside from that, a lot has changed over the past sixteen years. They now run a home remodeling business and The Rehab Life, a popular DIY channel on YouTube, Instagram and Facebook. On any given day, you can find them driving their Jeep Wranglers (#jeeplife) around the Twin Cities, going from the hardware store to their renovation projects to the studio where they shoot their tutorials. They love the variety their unique job brings, and whether it's negotiating a real estate deal, coming up with a new kitchen layout, staging a completed home, editing their YouTube videos (or writing this book!), they always bring their followers along for the ride.

FOLLOW THEIR JOURNEY AT:

YouTube: www.youtube.com/therehablife

Instagram: www.instagram.com/therehablife

Facebook: www.facebook.com/therehablife

# INDEX